PASS DEFENSE DRILLS

George Allen (*photograph by Vic Stein*)

PASS DEFENSE DRILLS

GEORGE H. ALLEN
Head Coach, Los Angeles Rams

ADDISON-WESLEY PUBLISHING COMPANY
Reading, Massachusetts · Menlo Park, California · London · Don Mills, Ontario

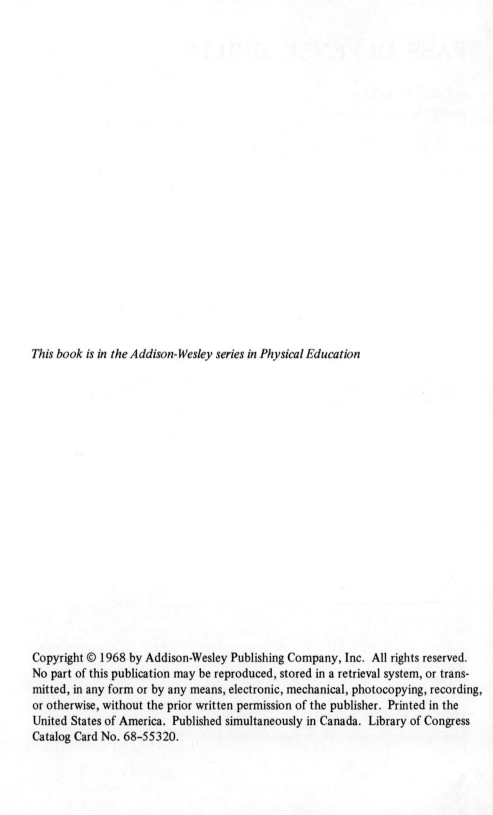

This book is in the Addison-Wesley series in Physical Education

ABOUT THE AUTHOR

George H. Allen is head coach of the Los Angeles Rams. In 1967 he was named
National Football League "Coach of the Year" by *Sporting News*, and received
similar honors from The Associated Press, United Press International, the Washington Touchdown Club, and several other organizations. He joined the Rams after
serving for 8 years as a defensive coach and personnel director with the Chicago
Bears under George S. Halas. In 1963 his Bears' defensive unit led the league in 10
of 18 categories, finishing second in 7 others, and third in the remaining category.
By allowing only 141 points in a 14-game schedule that season, the Bears under
Allen set an NFL record which may never be broken. His defense intercepted 41
passes in that one year.

Before his stint with the Bears, Allen spent 3 years as head coach at Morningside
College in Iowa, and 6 years as head coach at Whittier College in California. Each
of his head-coaching assignments has involved building losing teams into winners.
In 21 years of coaching, 11 of them as a head coach, he has seen only 5 losing
seasons.

Allen won 9 letters in high school, competing in football, basketball, and track.
He played college football at Alma and Marquette, and was a member of the wres-
tling team at the University of Michigan. He is a graduate of the University of
Michigan, where he earned both B.S. and M.A. degrees. He has advanced credits
toward his Ph.D. at the University of Southern California.

The author of four previous books on football drills, training, organization, and
scouting, Allen is recognized as one of the ablest teachers of the game, and is known
for his ability to bring out the best in his players. He is a member of Sigma Delta
Psi (the national athletic and academic fraternity) and is an honorary chief of the
Sioux Indian tribe.

v

To my three sons: George, Gregory, and Gerald. May they possess some of the fine qualities of character exemplified by the players I have had the privilege of coaching: determination, pride, loyalty, self-discipline, and ability.

ACKNOWLEDGMENTS

Any coach's reputation is built on the loyalty and skill of his players and colleagues. I wish to acknowledge the inspiration and help of the following:

The Los Angeles Rams secondary, led by Ed Meador, Irv Cross, Clancy Williams and Chuck Lamson.

The Rams linebackers, led by Maxie Baughan, Jack Pardee, Myron Pottios, and Doug Woodlief.

The Rams defensive line, led by David Jones, Merlin Olsen, Lamar Lundy, Roger Brown and Rosey Grier.

All the other men of our defensive unit, who comprise what I believe is the finest defensive unit in pro football.

Fritz Crisler, Bennie Oosterbaan, and Cliff Keen, my associates at the University of Michigan.

George S. Halas, owner and coach of the Chicago Bears, with whom I had a long association, and Clark Shaughnessy, formerly with the Bears.

My former defensive players with the Bears, led by Doug Atkins in the defensive line, Bill George, Larry Morris, Joe Fortunato, and Dick Butkus of the linebackers, and Richie Petitbon, Rosey Taylor, Bennie McRae, and Dave Whitsell of the secondary.

Last, but certainly not least, my college players: those at Morningside College, which was my first head coaching assignment, and those at Whittier College.

INTRODUCTION

In 1956, while I was coaching at Whittier College, I started gathering the material for this book. The original idea was to publish a book along the lines of my other two texts on football drills. *The Encyclopedia of Football Drills* and *Winning Football Drills* (published by Prentice-Hall) were the first books published on the organization of drills according to type. This present book was started while I was still coaching in college, and was completed at the end of this past season with the Los Angeles Rams.

I have coached football at the high school, college, and professional level, and have acted as both assistant coach and head coach. I have had assignments coaching offensive backs, offensive linemen, receivers, defensive linemen, defensive linebackers, and deep backs. The variety of experience has been most valuable to me. However, from the beginning, teaching pass defense has always been one of the most challenging tasks. In fact, I believe that the teaching of total pass defense is the most difficult assignment in coaching football, and that those players who specialize in pass defense have the most difficult positions to play.

Every coach needs good pass defense drills. A practice program is no better than the drills that go to make it up. Every drill must have a purpose, and must be performed under conditions as close to game conditions as possible. No coach should allow his players to perform drills carelessly or at a modified pace. *The way a player practices and the way he executes pass defense drills is the way he will usually perform in a game.*

Pass Defense Drills, therefore, is not just a textbook made up of pro football drills that I have used while on assignment with the Chicago Bears and the Los Angeles Rams. It is a text largely written for college football coaches and players. It also contains a sprinkling of drills which I believe are practical in all areas of football (high school, college, and pro). I hope that the coaches who read this text may find ideas that will be valuable in their own football programs.

July 1968   G. H. A.
Los Angeles, California

TABLE OF CONTENTS

CHAPTER 1

PREGAME DRILLS

The primary purpose of pregame drills is to warm up all the pass defenders. Deep backs, above all, must be loose and supple on the first play of the game. How many times have you seen a long pass completed on the very first play because the defender was a step slow? Many times this is the result of improper pregame warm-up drills.

The second purpose of pregame drills is to review a limited number of essential fundamentals. This warm-up period should provide practice for the deep backs in covering an offensive player while going at top speed. In addition, it gives them an opportunity to get the feel of the ball, the turf, the weather, etc.

The third purpose of pregame drills is primarily psychological. Make sure that you do *not* provide the pass defenders with difficult chances. Make them look good in every drill. In addition, be certain that your drills are well organized, and above all *do not wear them out* during this warm-up session.

SPEED DRILL

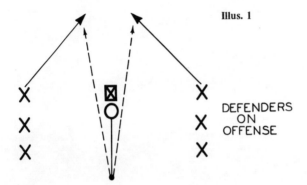

Illus. 1

DEFENDERS
ON
OFFENSE

The purpose of this drill is to provide a warm-up for the defensive backs, while at the same time allowing them to handle the ball as much as possible in a short interval.

INSTRUCTIONS

1. Have all the defenders form two lines on each side of the passer. Use a reserve quarterback if possible in this drill, with a center.

2. As quickly as the quarterback can throw, have the defenders release for a pass.

3. Have the quarterback throw only short passes, and let each defender place the ball on the ground next to the center as he returns.

4. Use plenty of footballs.

5. See Illustration 1.

Comment: This is a fine pregame drill when a team is playing in cold weather, because all the defensive backs are kept active. It is a rapid-fire drill, and it is amazing how many passes each defender can catch and how much running takes place within 2 or 3 minutes. This is also an excellent drill for offensive ends.

PITCH-AND-CATCH DRILL

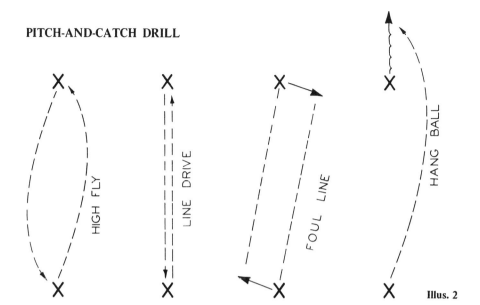

Illus. 2

The purpose of this drill is to provide extra practice in playing the ball for the deep backs and linebackers.

INSTRUCTIONS

1. Line up the defensive backs at an open end of the field so that plenty of space is available.

2. Provide one football for each pair of defensive backs. This allows for rapid-fire interceptions in a short space of time.

3. Have the players throw both long and short interceptions (see Glossary for a definition of this word as used here). In addition, have each defender play the ball on a couple of "alley oop" passes (see Glossary).

4. Let each defender call for the type of pass he wants to warm up on, and as many passes as he wishes.

5. Let the players perform this drill prior to returning to the locker room before the game commences, when the players are completely warm.

6. See Illustration 2.

Comment: The pitch-catch drill is primarily recommended as a pregame warm-up drill, but can be used to advantage at any time. Many times it is advantageous to allow the defensive backs to conduct the drill by themselves. Too many regimented drills are not desirable.

MACHINE-GUN DRILL

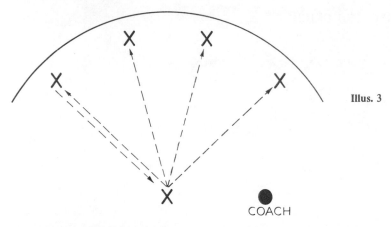

Illus. 3

This is a good drill for a defensive backfield coach who wants a drill that will develop competition among the defenders and aid in developing peripheral perception and quick hand reactions.

INSTRUCTIONS

1. Line up four defensive men in a half-moon formation. Let any one of the four hold a football.

2. Have the defensive back who will be "machine-gunned" stand 10 yards away and face the other four men. Let him also have a football.

3. When you give the command "Go," have the lone player throw the ball to any one of the four men facing him.

4. Simultaneously let one of the other four players fire the other ball to the lone player.

5. A rapid combat of "machine-gunning" with the footballs ensues. Tell the "gunner" not to throw the ball to a man who already has a ball.

6. The "gunner" must receive the ball without fumbling and must pass it while the second ball is on the way.

7. The instant that he fumbles a pass, he is out, and another player from the half-moon formation takes his place.

8. After all five men have had a chance to be "gunned," determine the highest score.

9. See Illustration 3.

Comment: This is another good pregame warm-up drill.

TWIN-CROSSING DRILL

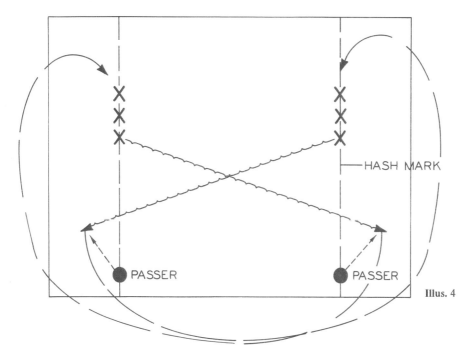

Illus. 4

The purpose of this drill is to give the players practice in intercepting the football while they are running forward, and in catching it at various angles.

INSTRUCTIONS

1. Have the defensive backs line up in two rows on their respective hash marks (see Glossary).

2. To avoid delays, arrange to have two passers and at least four footballs.

3. Have the line on the left break to the right, and the line on the right break to the left.

4. Get each player to continue on around to the end of the other line after intercepting the ball.

5. See Illustration 4.

Comment: This is a rapid-fire interception drill that provides action for all the defensive backs when practice time is limited.

CANNONBALL DRILL

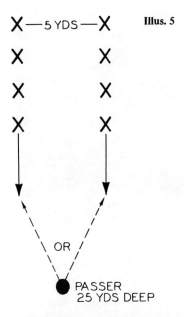

Illus. 5

The purpose of this drill is to give the players practice in intercepting a football that has been thrown very hard.

INSTRUCTIONS

1. Place the defenders in two separate lines, five yards apart, facing the passer.

2. Station a reserve quarterback at least 25 yards away from the front defender.

3. Get the defenders to run forward, but under control.

4. Have the quarterback throw cannonball passes to either defender; one catches the pass and the other continues straight on.

5. See Illustration 5.

FINAL-FILTER DRILL

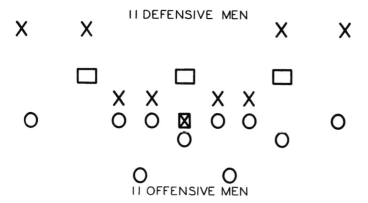

The purpose of this drill is to provide a final warm-up for the offense and defense before they go to the locker room.

INSTRUCTIONS

1. Have the offense use both runs and passes that they want to practice at this time.

2. Have the defense use defensive plays that are designed to stop the plays that the opponents are expected to use in this game.

3. Let the offense run its plays at top speed and the defense line accept the blocks coming across at half speed.

4. Tell the offensive ends and backs to run at full speed and the defensive backs to cover, but to allow the receivers to catch the ball.

5. Get the players to reverse directions after a few minutes, so that the passers throw both ways.

6. See Illustration 6.

Comment: This is a good warm-up that helps timing and allows some hitting by both units before the kickoff.

CHAPTER 2

FORMS AND CHARTS

Each defensive coach has his own ideas and way of using charts to assist him. Most charts and forms require constant revision if a coach is to keep up with the constant changes in offensive trends. The forms and charts given here are for the most part *not* designed to be used on the day of the game. The purpose of these charts is to assist both coach and player *before* the game.

The forms and charts in this chapter are intended to make the defensive player more conscious of vital statistics. In addition, they should be of some help in motivating the linebackers and deep backs.

Good defensive teams always take pride in their defensive ability.

TIME STUDY CHART

Number of minutes for each drill

	1st week				2nd week				3rd week				TOTAL
DATE													
FOOTWORK													
INDIVIDUAL PASS DEFENSE													
PLAYING THE BALL													
DEFLECTIONS													
INTERCEPTIONS													
RUNNING BACKWARD													
ONE-ON-ONE													
OUTNUMBERED													
TACKLING													
BALL FIGHTING													
BODY POSITION													

Illus. 7

The purpose of this chart is to keep a record of time devoted to various pass defense drills.

INSTRUCTIONS

1. Use the above pass defense time study chart; it is a valuable guide to a coach in determining the amount of time the secondary spends on drills.

2. See Illustration 7.

Comment: Pass defense drills are sometimes quite lengthy, and unless you organize them well, you may waste much time in practice sessions.

12   Forms and charts

WALL CHART

INTERCEPTION & BLOCKING CHART

PLAYER	TOTAL	OPPONENT	YDG.	ACCUM.	BLK.	PLAYER	TOTAL	T.D.

Illus. 8

The purpose of this wall chart is to provide the pass defenders with a visual aid to assessing their performance.

INSTRUCTIONS

1. Keep the wall chart accurate and current. This is important.

2. Place the chart in an area where everyone can view it. Make it large enough to be read from a distance.

3. Look at the sample headings for an accumulative chart given below.

4. See Illustration 8.

NAME OPPONENT BATTED BALLS INTERCEPTIONS BLOCKS YDS RET.

PASS TRAINING CARDS

The purpose of these cards is to illustrate every pass pattern that your opponents could employ.

INSTRUCTIONS

1. Diagram patterns used by your opponents on 14 x 18 white cards which have been punched with three holes.

2. Diagram every conceivable pass pattern on these training cards.

3. Have your players run the patterns against the defense until the defense has learned to cover all of them properly.

4. Use both sides of the training cards. Usually one or two patterns at a time are sufficient. Alternate cards every other day.

5. Use Junior Varsity to run patterns.

6. See the six variations given in Illustration 9.

Comment: This procedure is important during spring practice and early fall sessions.

PASS TRAINING CARDS

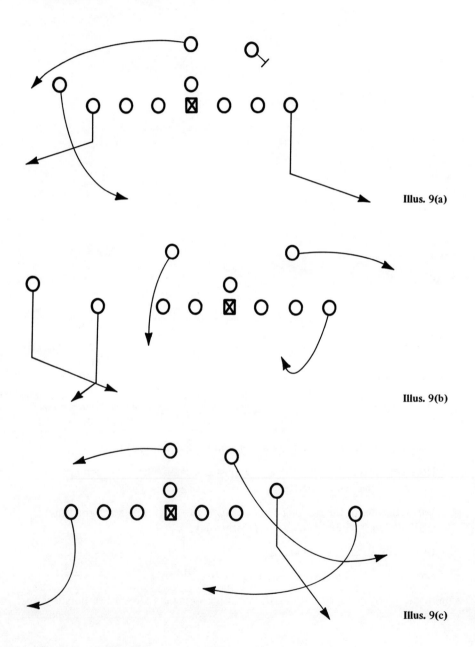

Illus. 9(a)

Illus. 9(b)

Illus. 9(c)

PASS TRAINING CARDS

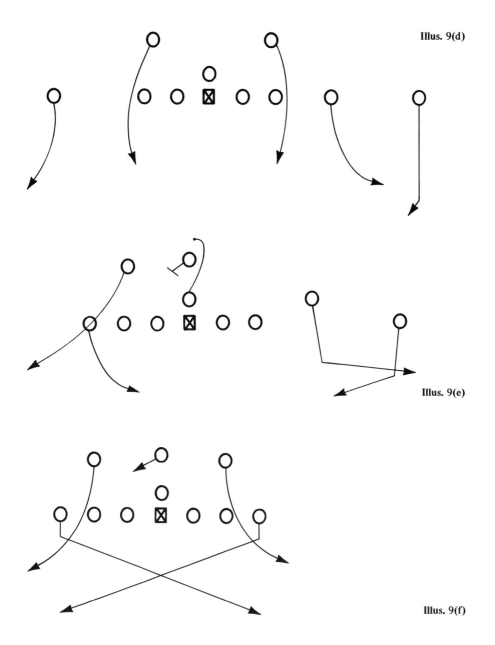

Illus. 9(d)

Illus. 9(e)

Illus. 9(f)

OPPONENTS' FORMATION CHARTS

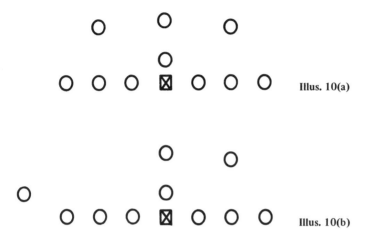

Illus. 10(a)

Illus. 10(b)

The purpose of this chart is to allow the linebackers and secondary to check their assignments against various formations.

INSTRUCTIONS

1. Diagram your opponents' formations on 14 x 18 white cards which have been punched with three holes.

2. See to it that the cards contain every formation that your defense might face during the entire season.

3. Use these cards first in the lecture hall so that the players can check their assignments and see how they need to adjust from one formation to another.

4. When you use the opponent formation cards on the field, have a complete offensive unit line up, but *do not* have them run any plays, because you are only identifying opponents' formations and checking your defense for alignment, adjustment, and assignment.

5. Give your players this type of training in spring practice or during the twice-a-day sessions in the fall.

6. See the ten sample formations in Illustration 10.

Comment: Since some of these formations are formations your team may never have to face, there is no need to run plays. However, by getting them prepared for a surprise you are helping the entire defensive unit psychologically.

OPPONENTS' FORMATION CHARTS

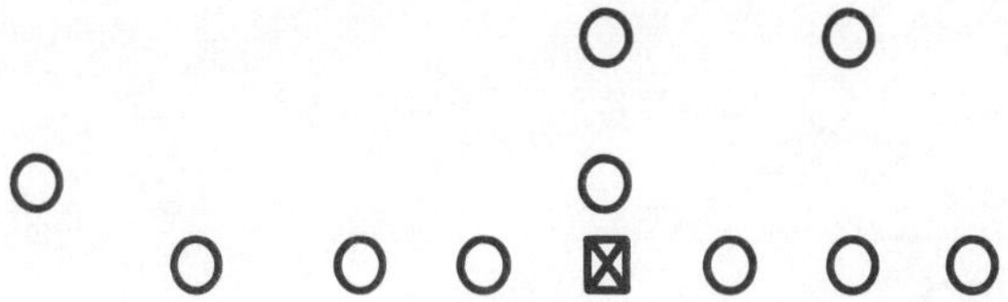

Illus. 10(c)

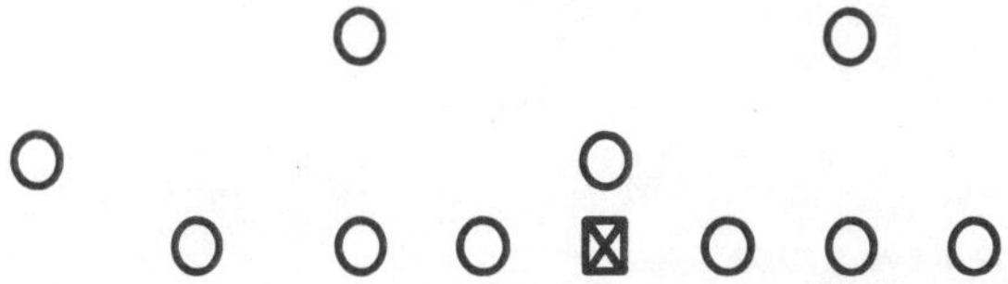

Illus. 10 (d)

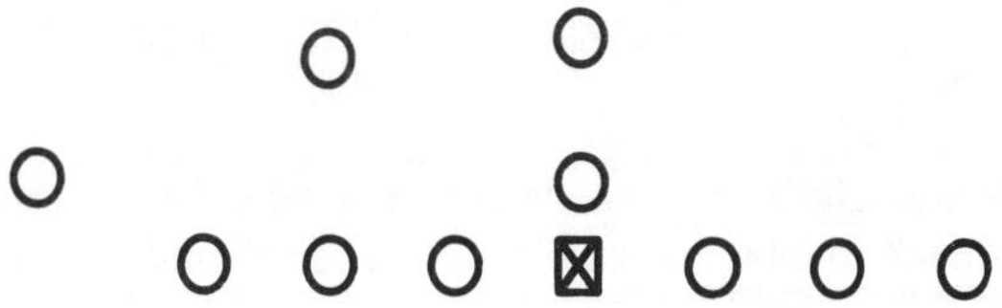

Illus. 10(e)

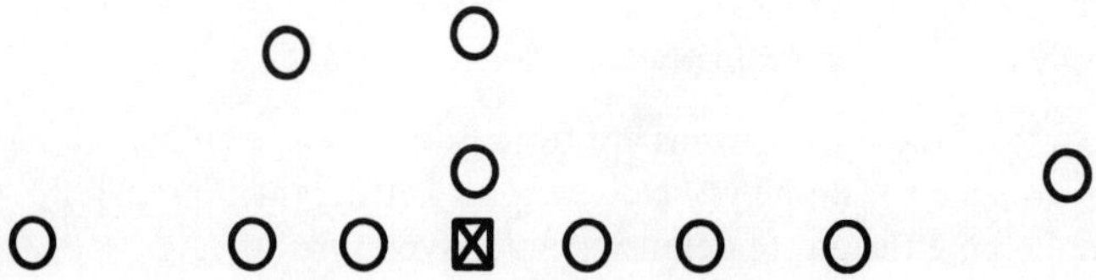

Illus. 10(f)

OPPONENTS' FORMATION CHARTS

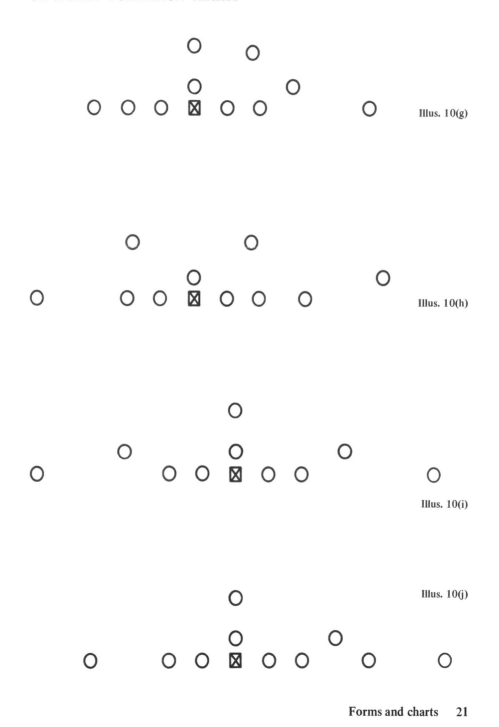

Illus. 10(g)

Illus. 10(h)

Illus. 10(i)

Illus. 10(j)

FIELD-OUTLINE DRILL

Illus. 11

SHORT OUTSIDE	SHORT MIDDLE	SHORT OUTSIDE
MEDIUM OUTSIDE	MEDIUM MIDDLE	MEDIUM OUTSIDE
DEEP OUTSIDE	DEEP MIDDLE	DEEP OUTSIDE

The purpose of this drill is to teach the concept of zone responsibilities to the entire secondary.

INSTRUCTIONS

1. Explain this first in a lecture hall, with blackboard and chalk, before going onto the field.

2. Have the groundskeeper line off the field into three zones separated by the hash marks.

3. See Illustration 11.

SPLIT-UP-THE-FIELD DRILL

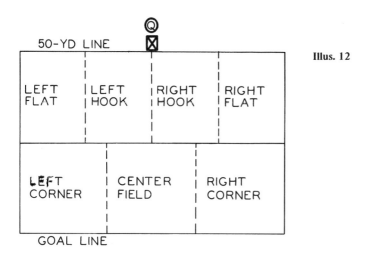

Illus. 12

The purpose of this chart is to divide up the field into four short zones and three deep zones.

INSTRUCTIONS

1. Before going out on the football field, first explain the zones to the players by means of lecture and blackboard.

2. To help the players learn their coverage, have the groundskeeper line the field into zones.

3. Use a center and quarterback to help the players get a feel for the proper distance of each zone from the center and quarterback.

4. See Illustration 12.

Comment: By splitting up the football field into seven zones, you help the players to better understand their responsibilities.

PASS-DEFENSE-POSITION DRILL

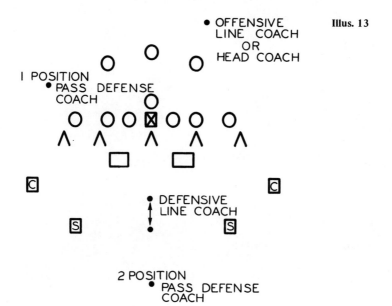

The purpose of this chart is to illustrate the correct spots for the defensive coach and his assistants to stand.

INSTRUCTIONS

1. The pass defense coach, in order to observe the entire pass pattern, should stand behind the offensive unit on either one side or the other.

2. Alternatively, the pass defense coach may stand downfield. But, to follow the coverage, he must be deeper than the deepest receiver. As a result, many times he is out of the picture because he is too deep. In addition, he cannot communicate effectively with his players and must run back and forth from the defensive huddle to his place downfield.

3. See Illustration 13.

Comment: We are all creatures of habit, and many times coaches will assume locations during practice that place them at a disadvantage.

PASS ZONE CHART

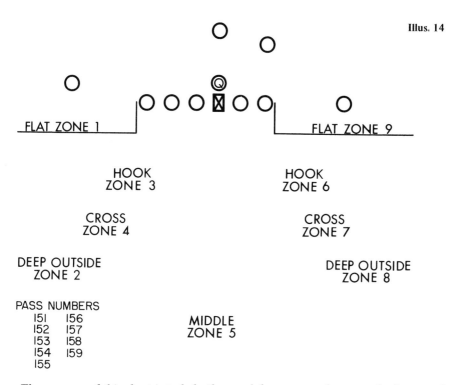

Illus. 14

FLAT ZONE 1   FLAT ZONE 9

HOOK
ZONE 3   HOOK
ZONE 6

CROSS
ZONE 4   CROSS
ZONE 7

DEEP OUTSIDE
ZONE 2   DEEP OUTSIDE
ZONE 8

PASS NUMBERS
151	156
152	157
153	158
154	159
155	

MIDDLE
ZONE 5

The purpose of this chart is to help the coach keep a complete record of runs and passes used by the opponent.

INSTRUCTIONS

1. Make out a chart using a numbering system similar to that used by your offense.

2. List passes by names or numbers in the bottom left portion of the chart.

3. See Illustration 14.

Comment: This chart can be useful at half-time, from either an offensive or defensive viewpoint.

EIGHT-ZONE CARD DRILL

The purpose of drawing up a card with eight zones is to outline the pass responsibilities of each player.

INSTRUCTIONS

1. Choose one or the other of the two formats given here.

2. Note that Card 1 consists of an offensive formation of seven linemen and the quarterback.

3. Note that Card 2 consists of an offensive formation of five linemen and the quarterback. (This is the card that is preferable.)

4. Write in the position of each defender, plus the type of pass he is responsible for in his zone.

5. Divide the card into as many zones as desirable.

6. See the two parts of Illustration 15 on opposite page.

PASS RESPONSIBILITY CARD

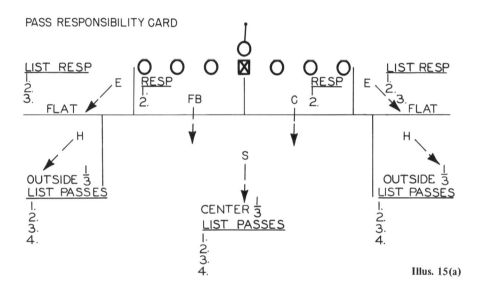

LIST RESP
1.
2.
3.
   FLAT

E   RESP
    1.
    2.

FB

C   RESP
    1.
    2.

E   LIST RESP
    1.
    2.
    3.
       FLAT

H

OUTSIDE $\frac{1}{3}$
LIST PASSES
1.
2.
3.
4.

S

CENTER $\frac{1}{3}$
LIST PASSES
1.
2.
3.
4.

H

OUTSIDE $\frac{1}{3}$
LIST PASSES
1.
2.
3.
4.

Illus. 15(a)

CARD 2

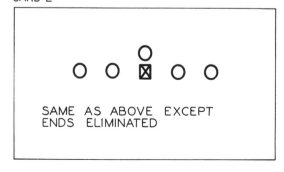

SAME AS ABOVE EXCEPT
ENDS ELIMINATED

Illus. 15(b)

STATISTICAL PASS CROSS-CHECKING DRILL

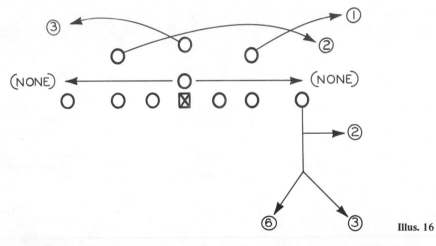

Illus. 16

The object of this chart is to enable the coach, after he has viewed film, to tabulate, on play charts, the pass routes of all receivers. In addition, he can use such a chart to present a summary of the running plays, indicating how many times runs were called to a certain spot.

INSTRUCTIONS

See Illustration 16.

OFFENSIVE WORK SHEET

The purpose of such a work sheet is to enable the defensive coach to check each defense against offensive variations.

INSTRUCTIONS

1. Make a work sheet or chart of the offensive team and list every offensive formation possible.

2. Next diagram the defenses against each of these offensive formations.

3. Third, list as many offensive variations as possible from each formation. Diagram each defense against all these variations.

4. When you have established sound rules for your men to use against each offensive formation, chart the defenses on large field cards.

5. Use part of each defensive practice session to work through the tactics the defense can use against some of these variations. Take a few at a time.

6. While you teach the defense, you should also teach the adjustments. In this manner, you can help the players obtain a total picture.

7. At the same time, teach any "automatic defenses" that are necessary whenever the specific defense does not apply.

DEEP-POSITION DRILL

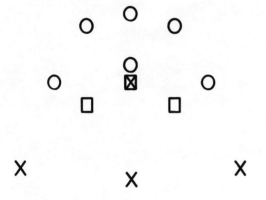

The purpose of this chart is to emphasize the fact that there is one position that affords the pass defense coach the best view.

INSTRUCTIONS

1. There are many positions that pass defense coaches assume. Some are good, while some could be improved.

2. One position that allows the coach to view everyone is the "deep position." If the coach stations himself downfield 35 yards, he can see both offense and defense.

3. If the pass defense coach stations himself too close he cannot see the patterns behind him, and as a result loses a total picture of the pass play.

4. See Illustration 17.

NUMBERED-ZONES DRILL

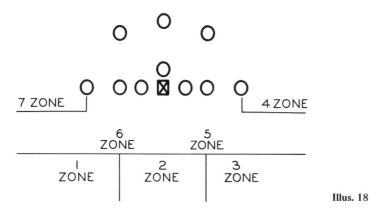

Illus. 18

The purpose of this chart is to provide a system whereby the coach can number each pass defense zone and indicate these zones on a chart so that the defenders can grasp the situation at a glance.

INSTRUCTIONS

1. Numbering the zones enables the coach to keep account of who is at fault on pass plays. It also shows players which zones are *not* to be occupied.

2. Such a chart serves as a teaching aid for the defenders. It helps them to learn their responsibilities on each kind of pass play.

3. See Illustration 18.

CHAPTER 3

REACTION DRILLS

Reaction is a composite skill. Quick hands and feet, good peripheral vision, timing, and body balance are reaction qualities that are necessary for deep backs. *On pass defense, reaction is everything.* This is one phase of defensive play that can be improved appreciably by using selected reaction drills.

There comes a time when any deep back, no matter how many other qualities he possesses, will either succeed or fail according to his defensive reaction ability. The only way defenders will improve and develop is through constant drilling. Individual drills are essential; they are better than team drills. After all, no pass defense is any stronger than any one individual's weakness, although this comment is not intended to minimize the importance of team drills.

Because many reaction drills are interchangeable with interception drills, deflection drills, playing-the-ball drills, and position-on-the-receiver drills, only drills that are especially designed to improve total reaction are included in this chapter.

When selecting a drill, the coach should always choose the drill or drills that will allow the defender to perform more than one movement. This is the secret of good drilling and proper drill selection.

BLIND DRILL

DEFENDERS' BACKS TO PASSERS

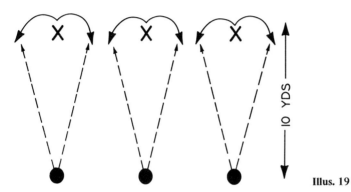

Illus. 19

The purpose of this drill is to teach the defenders to pivot quickly and sharpen their reactions so that they can intercept the ball.

INSTRUCTIONS

1. Station two, three, or four defenders ten yards apart, with the players that are to receive the ball having their backs turned to the passers.

2. Provide one football for each pair of players.

3. Upon a predetermined signal, let the passers throw their balls and at the same time let the defenders pivot quickly, trying to locate the football and intercept, if possible.

4. Let the players who are passing the ball gradually increase their distance from the defenders.

5. Have them throw all types of passes; each defender should take four turns before he goes on offense.

6. See Illustration 19.

Comment: This is a drill that the deep backs can practice among themselves. It enables a player to practice getting the ball in range of vision quickly without being able to follow it in flight from the passer's hands.

FIGHTING-FOR-THE-BALL DRILL

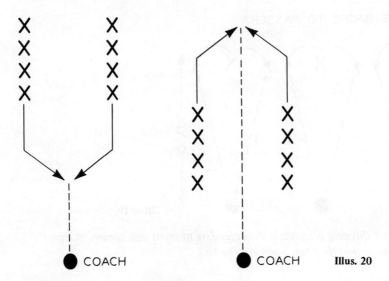

COACH   COACH   Illus. 20

The purpose of this drill is to teach the players to meet physical contact and fight for the ball.

INSTRUCTIONS

1. Line up the defenders in pairs and have them face the coach.

2. Have one player from each line run forward as you "lay" the ball in the air.

3. To increase competition, place players who are battling for the same position opposite each other.

4. You can vary this drill by having players line up in the same manner and then having them run backward. Since they are going away from the passer, they have to adjust to this when they are fighting for the ball.

5. See Illustration 20.

Comment: The teaching points of this drill are: timing of the jump, playing the ball at its highest point with arms elevated in front, use of hips and body for position, and actually fighting for the football.

FALLING-DOWN DRILL

The purpose of this drill is to try to prepare the defender for a miscue.

INSTRUCTIONS

1. Have the defensive players go through their various drills on footwork, covering all types of passes. These drills are to be done by vocal commands from you.

2. When you give the command "fall," the defender goes to the ground, and then quickly recovers and continues with the drill.

3. See how fast and how much you can lead your defenders to improve by means of this drill.

Comment: Many times a pass defender will slip and fall but not recover in time. He may think that, because he fell, he does not have a chance to make the play. But, with practice, defenders learn that they can slip and fall, then bounce up, and still be in position.

AROUND-THE-HORN DRILL

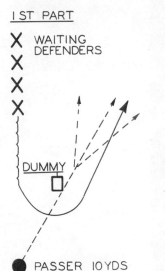

I ST PART

X WAITING
   DEFENDERS

X

X

X

DUMMY

PASSER 10 YDS
FROM DUMMY   **Illus. 21(a)**

The purpose of this drill is to train the defender to catch a ball at an angle while he is running backward. This is a reaction drill that prepares him for situations that he often has to meet in games when he is retreating and the ball is slightly off target.

INSTRUCTIONS

1. Line up your defenders and station a passer and a standing dummy as shown in the three diagrams (Illustration 21), which show the three parts of this drill.

2. Have a defender run forward and circle the standing dummy, then retreat rapidly, using proper footwork.

3. Let the passer either throw a pass directly at the defender, or to the right of him, or to the left, or sometimes short, so that the defender must backtrack.

4. In part two of the drill, get the passer to throw a wobbly pass, just as a passer often has to do during a game when he is rushed and throws a "ruptured duck" (see Glossary).

5. In part three, have the passer throw the ball underhand and low while the defender is going backward.

6. See the three parts of Illustration 21.

Comment: This is a difficult drill, and one that requires good timing by the passer, who is stationed 10 yards deep.

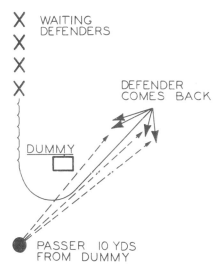

2 ND PART   CRAZY SPIN

X   WAITING
X   DEFENDERS
X
X

DEFENDER
COMES BACK

DUMMY

PASSER 10 YDS
FROM DUMMY

Illus. 21(b)

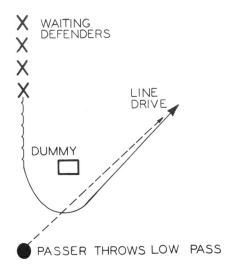

3 RD PART   LOW DRILL

X   WAITING
X   DEFENDERS
X
X

LINE
DRIVE

DUMMY

PASSER THROWS LOW PASS

Illus. 21(c)

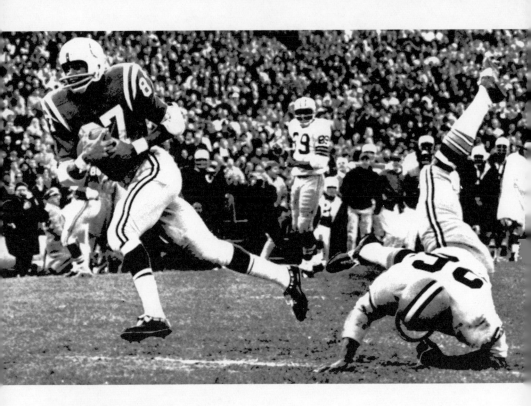

STOPWATCH DRILL

The purpose of this drill is to find out how fast your pass defenders can run backward.

INSTRUCTIONS

1. Have all your pass defenders (including linebackers) run 15 yards backward and make one complete turn.

2. Time all of them with a stopwatch. A time of 2.3 seconds is very good time.

3. Impress on them that some boys who are fast when they run forward can be beaten by a slower man when they are running backward.

4. Encourage them by assuring them that some defensive players, after they have mastered the technique of running backward, get so adept that they can run almost as fast backward as forward.

Comment: Most football coaches time their players in sprints, the distance varying from 20, 30, 40, 50, to a few hundred yards, and therefore know their speed in running forward. However, few coaches know what their pass defenders can do running backward.

REACTION DRILL

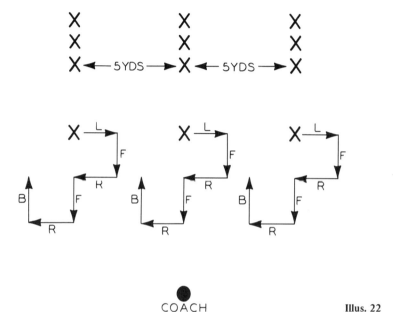

COACH   Illus. 22

The purpose of this drill is to improve the reactions of the defensive backs.

INSTRUCTIONS

1. Station three defensive backs facing you. They should be 5 yards apart to allow enough space to maneuver.

2. Start the drill by having the players run in place, and then give the following five commands: (a) front, (b) back, (c) left, (d) right, (e) down. When you say "Down," have them hit the ground and bounce up, running in place as fast as possible.

3. Insist that all movements be run at right angles. Do not let the players run in an arc.

4. As players progress, notice how much more territory they can cover between commands.

5. See Illustration 22.

COVERING-THE-FLAT DRILL

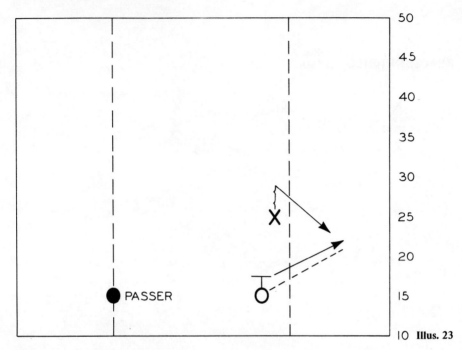

50

45

40

35

30

25

20

15

10 **Illus. 23**

The purpose of this drill is to give the defensive halfbacks practice in coming up and covering a delayed pass in the flat zone.

INSTRUCTIONS

1. Place a halfback on defense. Locate him 8-10 yards deep.

2. Station a center and passer on offense, with one receiver.

3. As the passer drops back to throw, let the defender retreat, slowly at first and then faster.

4. After the defender has retreated at least 5 yards, have the passer try to release the football.

5. Have the receiver do one of three things: (a) Delay in the flat zone and catch a pass over his outside shoulder. (b) Release immediately into the flat zone. (c) Fake going into the flat zone and try to get behind the halfback.

6. Get the defender to practice until he no longer takes that *extra step or two* backward before he comes forward; these backward steps usually place him in a bad position to break up the pass or make the tackle.

7. See Illustration 23.

LONG-ARM-ACTION DRILL

The purpose of this drill, which is really five drills in one, is to train the defenders to study the actions of the passer. Every passer makes a definite motion when he prepares to throw; we call this long arm action.

INSTRUCTIONS

1. Station two Junior Varsity players to act as posts. At first position them 10 yards apart. Gradually increase this distance to 12 yards, 15 yards, or more, as the defender improves.

2. Have a quarterback in this drill fake a pass one, two, or three times and then throw downfield 10 yards to a post man. Later have the quarterback move back to 15 yards.

3. Have the defender try to intercept the ball, and keep the quarterback from getting it to the post men.

4. Tell the passer never to fake more than three times, and usually only twice, because he will not have this long a time before he throws the ball during a game.

5. Have the defender keep his weight forward and feet moving, so that he can react quickly.

6. As a variation, start the defender 4 yards from the passer, and as the quarterback retreats let the defender go backward at the same time. This provides training in footwork plus practice in playing the ball and intercepting when possible. Still another variation is to use two defenders and three post men.

7. See the five parts of Illustration 24 on pages 42 and 43.

Comment: It is surprising how many players do not even come close to the ball when they first start doing this drill. This drill offers the coach a quick survey as to who can react and who cannot. It is also a good drill for linebackers. This is one of the finest drills in football, and is a must drill two or three times per week.

LONG-ARM-ACTION DRILL

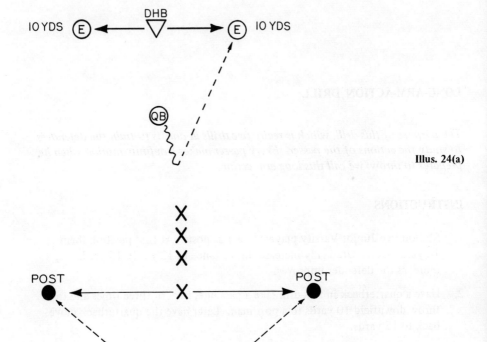

Illus. 24(a)

Illus. 24(b)

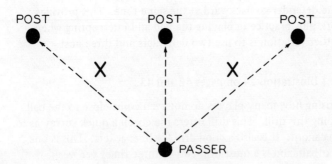

3 POSTS

Illus. 24(c)

4 POSTS

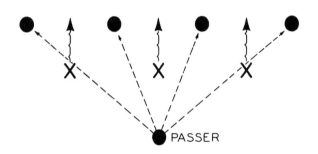

PASSER

Illus. 24(d)

2 POSTS

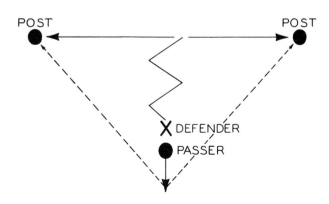

POST   POST

DEFENDER

PASSER

Illus. 24(e)

MACHINE-GUN DRILL

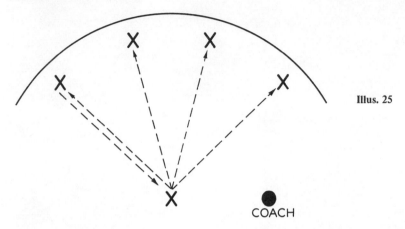

Illus. 25

This a good drill for a defensive backfield coach who wants a drill that will develop competition among the defenders and aid in developing peripheral perception and quick hands and reactions.

INSTRUCTIONS

1. Place four defensive men in a half-moon formation. Let any one of the four hold a football.

2. Have the defensive back who will be "machine-gunned" stand ten yards away and face the other four men. Let him also have a football.

3. When you give the command "go," the lone player throws the ball to any one of the four men facing him.

4. Simultaneously one of the other four players fires the other ball to the lone player.

5. A rapid combat of "machine-gunning" with the footballs ensues. Tell the "gunner" not to throw the ball to a man who already has one.

6. The lone "gunner" must receive the ball without fumbling and must pass it while the second ball is on the way.

7. The instant that he fumbles a pass, he is out, and another player from the half-moon formation takes his place.

8. After all five men have had a chance to be "gunned," determine the highest score.

9. See Illustration 25.

Comment: This is another good pregame warm-up drill.

FIRE DRILL

The purpose of this drill, which has four separate parts, is to teach running backward and playing the ball.

INSTRUCTIONS

1. First, station the deep backs in a single line and have them run backward for speed alone. Ten yards is adequate.

2. Second, have them run backward along a straight line and make three turns as they follow the line.

3. Third, have them run forward around you and follow your signals to turn right, left, etc.

4. Fourth, give each defender a football.

5. Have each defender run forward and hand the ball to you as he makes his turn.

6. Have each man, as he continues running around you, turn and run backward as fast as possible.

7. Have each defender yell "Pass, pass!" as he retreats, and make him concentrate on the ball.

8. Throw left, right, short, or deep, and let the defender try to intercept.

9. Get each defender to sprint back to his place in line with the football, and await his next turn.

10. See the four parts of Illustration 26.

Comment: This drill is for all the defensive backs.

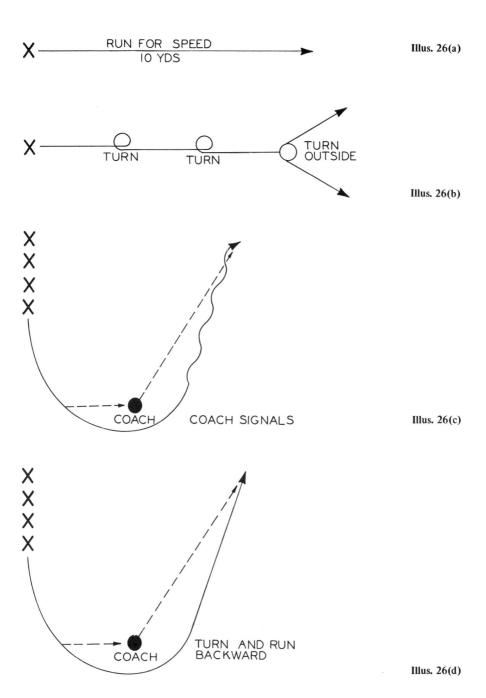

X —————— RUN FOR SPEED —————▶   Illus. 26(a)
10 YDS

X ——○—— TURN ——○—— TURN ——○ TURN OUTSIDE   Illus. 26(b)

COACH   COACH SIGNALS   Illus. 26(c)

COACH   TURN AND RUN BACKWARD   Illus. 26(d)

Reaction drills   47

CROSSBAR DRILL

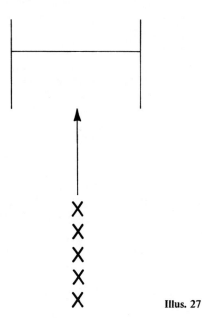

Illus. 27

The purpose of this drill is to provide practice for the defensive backs in getting off the ground.

INSTRUCTIONS

1. Have all the defensive backs line up, single file.

2. Have them run at three-quarter speed under the goal post and jump to touch the crossbar, first with the right hand and then with the left hand.

3. See Illustration 27.

Comment: This is a good drill to improve jumping, and the deep backs can readily see the degree to which they have improved by realizing how far they can get their hands over or around the crossbar. This is a fast-moving drill, and should be performed from both directions. It is also a drill that is good for morale.

TOTAL-REFLEX DRILL

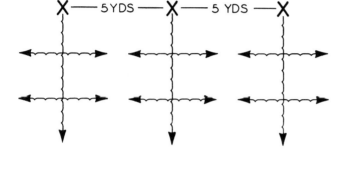

● COACH

Illus. 28

The purpose of this drill is to improve the reactions of the defensive backs.

INSTRUCTIONS

1. Station three defensive backs facing you. They should be 5 yards apart to allow enough space to maneuver.

2. Start the drill by having the players run in place, and then give the following five commands: (a) front, (b) back, (c) left, (d) right, (e) down. When you say "Down," have them hit the ground and bounce up, running in place as fast as possible.

3. Insist that all movements be run at right angles. Do not let the players run in an arc.

4. As players progress, notice how much more territory they can cover between commands.

5. See Illustration 28.

CHAPTER 4

FOOTWORK DRILLS

No matter how much speed a defensive back is inherently capable of, he still needs drills to develop and improve his footwork. Practicing bedrock fundamentals of footwork is a laborious task, but one that will eventually produce desirable results.

Footwork, although some coaches place little emphasis on it, is a vital bread-and-butter skill that every good pass defender must master. Fortunately it is one fundamental that can be vastly improved through proper teaching.

Proficient pass defenders are not born. They are made, as a result of a step-by-step process of teaching and practicing. It is true that some defenders are gifted with speed and are more agile than others. Nevertheless, all deep backs can hasten their development by constant drilling under supervision of the pass defense coach.

The following drills, in addition to teaching pass defenders proper footwork, will help body balance and quickness.

STANCE DRILL

 COACH   Illus. 29

The purpose of this drill is to check the defensive players' stance.

INSTRUCTIONS

1. Station the left halfbacks, right halfbacks, and safety men at their respective positions.

2. At the command "Ready," have the defenders take their defensive stances.

3. Check each man's stance, then make any comments you feel are necessary.

4. In order to avoid poor habits of stance, check the defensive players' stance frequently during the drill period.

5. See Illustration 29.

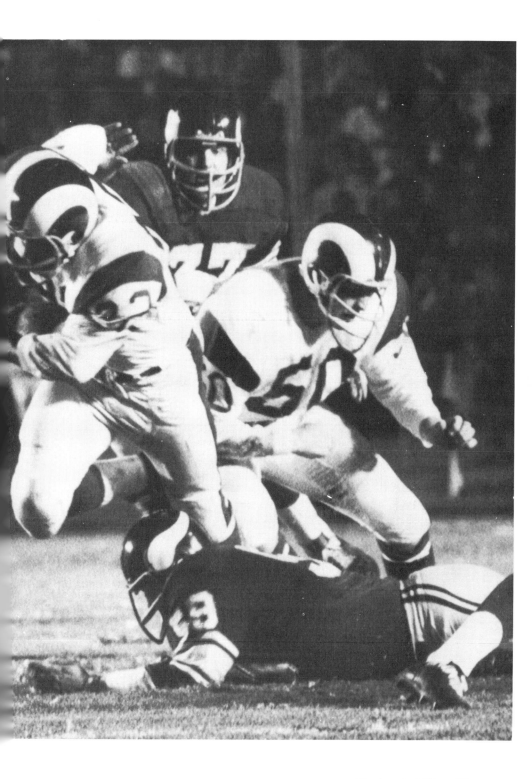

DOWN-THE-LINE DRILL

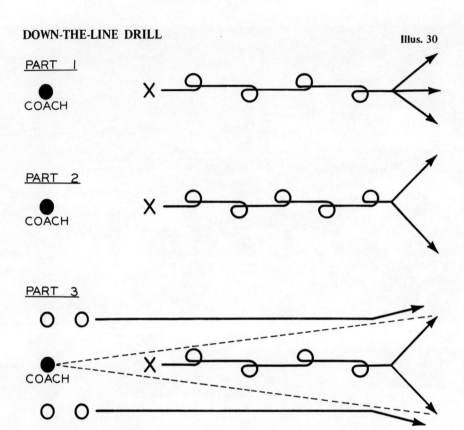

The object of this drill, which is really four drills in one, is to teach stance, take-off, footwork, and interceptions.

INSTRUCTIONS

1. Station a defender on one of the yard lines; you stand approximately 5 yards in front of him.

2. Have the defender retreat from you, along the yard line, using any one of the varied methods that a defender uses to retreat, running backward, turning, etc.

3. Start the drill at one-quarter speed to allow everyone to get the feel of the drill, since some players may be rather tight in the hips to start with.

4. Indicate by hand motions which way you want the defender to turn. After he has made four turns, keep him going in one direction for about 10 yards. Then get him to come back, get in line, and await his turn. (See Part 1 of Illustration 30.)

5. Next use a football in the drill. Again get the defender to retreat from you, weaving and turning but staying on the line. After indicating five or six turns by motions with the football, arc the ball so that the defender can reach it and intercept it at its highest point. (See Part 2 of Illustration 30.)

6. Occasionally throw the ball over the player's opposite shoulder; that is, start the defender going back to his right and then throw the ball over his left shoulder. Here you can allow him to turn his back to the passer and gain a step on the ball, even though this means that he cannot watch the ball in flight all the way.

7. After your defenders have improved, place a couple of dummies downfield 12 yards, and about 10 yards apart. Now throw a football at either dummy and tell the defender to try to intercept.

8. The final part of this drill is to station two receivers about 8 yards apart, with the defender stationed in front of you, as before. Have the receivers start downfield and throw the ball to either one. Let the retreating defender in the middle try to intercept the ball. Increase distance as the defender improves.

9. Here you want the defender to play the ball and *not* the receiver. If he is a step slow it is usually because he is playing the receiver more than he is the ball.

10. See the three parts of Illustration 30.

Comment: This is one of our favorite drills.

ADVANCED DOWN-THE-LINE DRILL

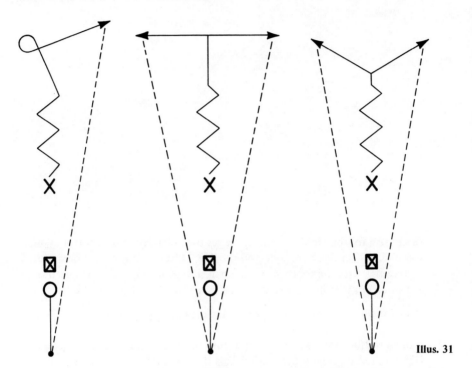

Illus. 31

The purpose of this drill is to give defensive backs an advanced drill after they have mastered the proper footwork. This drill follows the previous one and is a good variation.

INSTRUCTIONS

1. Position the defensive back facing the passer and 6 yards away from him. As the passer sets up, let the defender retreat as fast as possible, using the kind of footwork you want him to.

2. Instead of having the defender continue down the line as in the previous drills, have him cover outs, both right and left. Let the passer pass to both corners, and finally throw deep behind the defender when he is turned, making him turn like an outfielder to play the ball.

3. See Illustration 31.

TWO-MEN-DOWN-THE-LINE DRILL

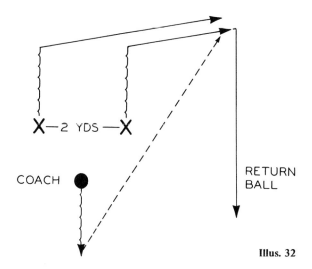

Illus. 32

The purpose of this drill is to enable players to practice footwork, body position, and intercepting the football.

INSTRUCTIONS

1. Station two players side by side approximately 2 yards apart.

2. Assuming that you are acting as a quarterback, drop back to pass. Let the defenders retreat. Throw to either player, and have the other one try to break up the pass or intercept.

3. The defenders will read your eyes because you will look right or left, deep or short.

4. Keep in mind that the coaching points of this drill are stance, footwork while going back, body position, playing the ball as its highest point with two hands, intercepting the ball, and returning the ball.

5. See Illustration 32.

ONE-ON-ONE DRILL

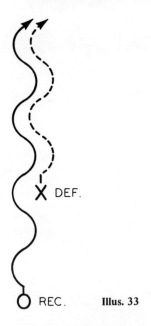

DEF.

REC.   **Illus. 33**

The purpose of this drill is to get defenders to practice footwork against an offensive receiver.

INSTRUCTIONS

1. Assign a defender to play defense. Tell him to keep to the lines, so that any deviation in his footwork will be easily noticed.

2. Locate an offensive end approximately 7 or 8 yards in front of the defensive back.

3. Let the offensive end run forward, as though he is trying to get to a spot where he will be in the open to receive a pass. Let him try to evade the defensive player, while still keeping to the lines.

4. Have the defender try to keep the offensive player from getting any closer to him than 3 yards, and concentrate only on the receiver. He must stay with the offensive player for at least 20 yards.

5. See Illustration 33.

Comment: This is a wonderful early-season drill, and one that should be repeated during the fall campaign to keep the pass defenders sharp.

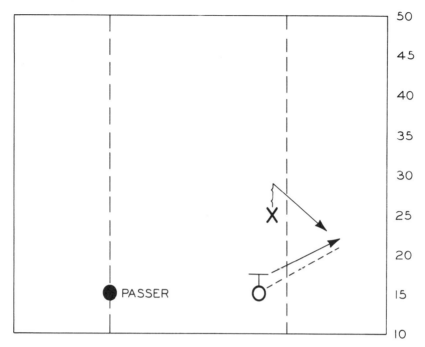

The purpose of this drill is to give the defensive halfbacks practice in coming up and covering a delayed pass into the flat zone.

INSTRUCTIONS

1. Station a halfback on defense. Locate him 8 to 10 yards deep.

2. Station a center and passer on offense, with one receiver.

3. As the passer drops back to throw, let the defender retreat, slowly at first and then faster.

4. After the defender has retreated at least 5 yards, have the passer try to release the football.

5. Have the receiver do one of three things: (a) Delay in the flat zone and catch a pass over his outside shoulder. (b) Run immediately into the flat zone. (c) Fake going into the flat zone and try to get behind the halfback.

6. Get the defender to practice until he no longer takes that *extra step or two* backward before he comes forward; these backward steps usually place him in a bad position to break up the pass or make the tackle.

7. See Illustration 34.

RUNNING-SQUARE-CORNERS DRILL

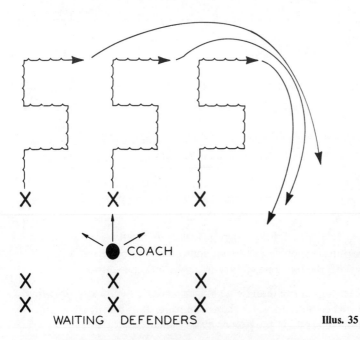

Illus. 35

The purpose of this drill is to help players improve footwork and body balance.

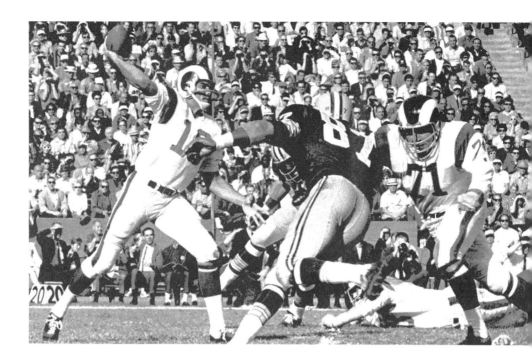

INSTRUCTIONS

1. Station three halfbacks on defense in their normal positions. These men should always assume their correct stance; do not start the drill until they have done so.

2. Take up a position 5 yards in front of the defenders. When you give a signal, have them start backward and move in the direction designated by your hand signals.

3. When the players are going away from you, the procedure is the same as in the down-the-line drill. When you signal a man to go to his right and he is going back looking over his left shoulder, he must *push off* on his *right foot,* squaring the corner, and sprint to his right in a straight line, etc.

4. Have players both run backward away from you and run away from you in a forward direction, looking back at you over their shoulders so that they know when to change directions.

5. As the players change directions, stress the important fundamentals: staying low, taking short steps, pivoting quickly, and planting the proper foot.

6. Give the players practice in suddenly coming forward after they have been running backward. They have to do this so often during actual games that they need practice if they are to eliminate false steps at such a time.

7. See Illustration 35.

CARIOCA DRILL

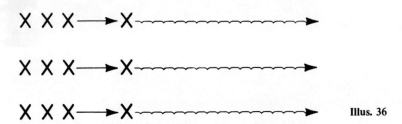

Illus. 36

The purpose of this drill is to enable players to practice footwork and to develop agility, coordination, and balance.

INSTRUCTIONS

1. Have the defensive backs line up in three lines, single file. Using three lines keeps everyone active.

2. To start the drill, have the players assume correct defensive stance.

3. Players are to move laterally for 15 yards, and then back again. The footwork is as follows: Cross the right foot in front of the left, keeping the left foot planted. Then move the left foot to the left laterally. Cross the right foot behind the left. Continue in this manner, alternately passing the right foot in front of the left and passing it behind the left.

4. After the players have gone 15 yards, have them return in the opposite direction, using the same step, but this time alternately crossing the left foot in front of the right and behind the right.

5. See Illustration 36.

REACH DRILL

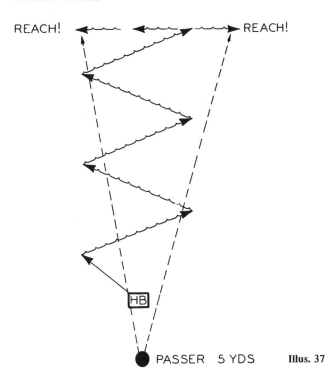

REACH!   REACH!

PASSER 5 YDS   Illus. 37

The purpose of this drill is to see how much ground one defender can cover, and to check his footwork.

INSTRUCTIONS

1. Station one defensive player in the position he normally plays on defense.

2. Have the passer fake passes three, four, or five times, and then throw the ball within range of the defender.

3. The passer should throw the ball so that the defensive back can just reach it each time if his body mechanics and reaction time are good.

4. For this drill, use a quarterback rather than a coach; have the quarterback, at the start of the drill, be 5 yards from the defensive player.

5. See Illustration 37.

CHANGING-DIRECTION DRILL

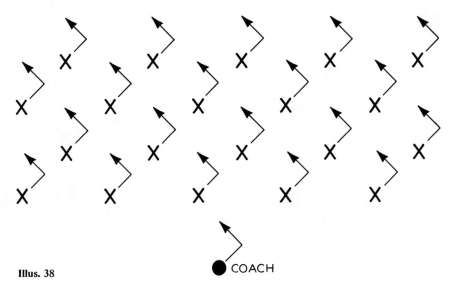

Illus. 38

COACH

The purpose of this drill is to teach the defensive backs and linebackers to move backward rapidly and to change direction without taking their eyes off the ball.

INSTRUCTIONS

1. Form all the defensive backs and linebackers into 4 or 5 lines facing you.

2. Take up a position 10 to 15 yards away, and facing the defenders.

3. Move toward them and fake a pass to your right. The pass defenders will move to their left.

4. Next fake a pass to your left, and the defenders will change directions.

5. After the defenders have changed directions several times, throw the ball. When one of them intercepts it, the others should form interference and run the ball back to the starting point.

6. See Illustration 38.

LATERAL-MOVEMENT DRILL

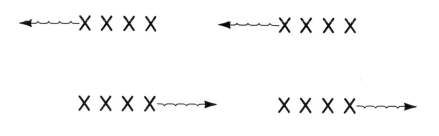

Illus. 39   ● COACH

The purpose of this drill is to get players to practice footwork while running in a lateral direction.

INSTRUCTIONS

1. Divide the defensive backs into two groups. Assuming that there are 16 pass defenders, divide the players into two units of eight each.

2. Use both hand motions and voice in this drill.

3. You are to represent a passer. On a signal from you, let the backs go 5 or 10 yards to their right or to their left, and return on another signal from you. Have the two groups of defenders go in opposite directions.

4. See Illustration 39.

Comment: This is a good early-season drill to check footwork.

OUTSIDE DRILL

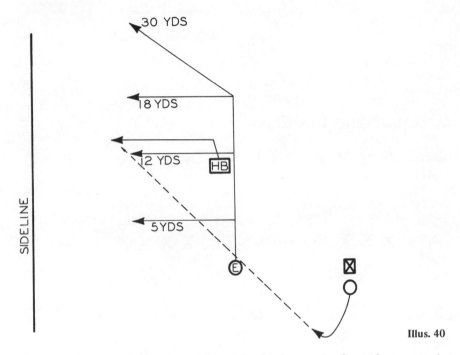

Illus. 40

The purpose of this drill is to combine all the fundamentals of outside coverage in one drill.

INSTRUCTIONS

1. Station a receiver on offense, with a passer.

2. Use one defender at a time. Make him responsible for short-out, medium-out, deep-out, and flag maneuvers.

3. Have the receiver limit his moves to the above four. He may use any one.

4. Until the defender has mastered his footwork on the four patterns, you can also use this drill without a receiver. Then add an offensive end and repeat.

5. See Illustration 40.

PARALLEL DRILL

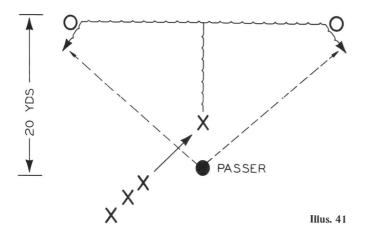

Illus. 41

The purpose of this drill is to have players practice breaking for a thrown ball at lateral angles.

INSTRUCTIONS

1. Station two offensive ends 20 yards downfield, facing the quarterback, or passer.

2. Have the defensive back assume his stance and then start backward, using whatever footwork you want him to.

3. When the defender has gone back about 15 or 20 yards, have him straighten up.

4. Let the quarterback throw the ball to either offensive end.

5. Have the defender try to break parallel to the offensive ends, facing in the right direction, and then try to move into the ball.

6. See Illustration 41.

DOG-EAT-DOG DRILL

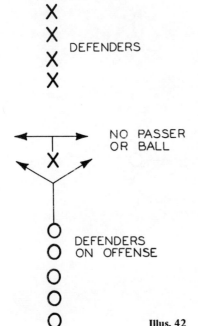

Illus. 42

Many times it is necessary to practice pass coverage when there are no offensive personnel present. The object of this drill is to enable defenders to practice pass defense when only the deep backs are available.

INSTRUCTIONS

1. Split the defenders into two equal groups, placing half on defense and the other half on offense.

2. Station the defenders 6 to 8 yards from the first offensive man.

3. Have the offensive player go downfield at three-quarter speed and break to his right or left.

4. Let the defensive man try to cover him. Do not use a football in this drill.

5. After the offensive player runs a pattern, let him go to the rear of the defensive line and have the defender take his place at the end of the offensive column.

6. See Illustration 42.

TEN-YARD PASS DEFENSE DRILL

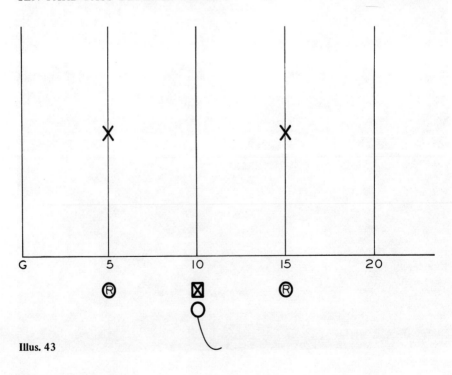

Illus. 43

The object of this drill is to begin teaching pass defense without giving the offensive man the advantage.

INSTRUCTIONS

1. Station a passer, center, and two receivers on offense on the sideline, one on the 5-yard line and the other on the 15-yard line. This is a cross-field drill.

2. Place two defenders 8 yards deep, one on the 5-yard line and the other on the 15-yard line.

3. Let the receivers have a limited area in which to maneuver. One receiver has the area between the goal line and the 10-yard line; the other receiver has the area between the 15- and the 25-yard line.

4. Let the receiver who takes the pass try to get free and let the defender work the 5-yard line (or the 15-yard line) back and forth.

5. When the defender improves, add 5 yards, and then 10 yards to the area in which he and the receiver may maneuver.

6. Alternate receivers at first, and then place two defenders versus two receivers.

7. See Illustration 43.

Comment: This is a good drill to build confidence in the defensive backs.

STOPWATCH DRILL

The purpose of this drill is to find out how fast your pass defenders can run backward.

INSTRUCTIONS

1. Have all your pass defenders (including linebackers) run 15 yards backward and make one complete turn.

2. Time all of them with a stopwatch. A time of 2.3 seconds is very good time.

3. Impress on them that some boys who are fast when they run forward can be beaten by a slower man when they are running backward.

4. Encourage them by assuring them that some defensive players, after they have mastered the technique of running backward, get so adept that they can run almost as fast backward as forward.

Comment: Most football coaches time their players in sprints, the distance varying from 20, 30, 40, 50, to a few hundred yards, and therefore know their speeds in running forward. However, few coaches know what their pass defenders can do running backward.

CHAPTER 5

INTERCEPTION DRILLS

One of the greatest and most spectacular plays in football is a pass interception. Intercepting a forward pass is a work of art, and is a specialized skill consisting of perfect timing, coordination, relaxed hands, and footwork ability. It is one of the most difficult skills in football to master. A pass defender running backward is required to cover a greyhound receiver running forward. In addition, the receiver knows where he is going because he has a predetermined route, but the defender naturally does not know this prearranged course.

Deep backs rarely get enough drilling time to work on this phase of pass defense. *The defenders must drill on interceptions just as the offensive ends work on receiving.* Statistics indicate that most interceptions are made while a defender is coming forward into the football. Normally there is a clash of hand and ball unless the defender has sufficient training. This is not a problem on offense, because both the ball and the receiver are going in the same direction.

This chapter contains fifteen interception drills that will ensure maximum dividends from the time devoted to this important skill of pass defense.

74   Interception drills

PLAYING-THE-FIELD DRILL

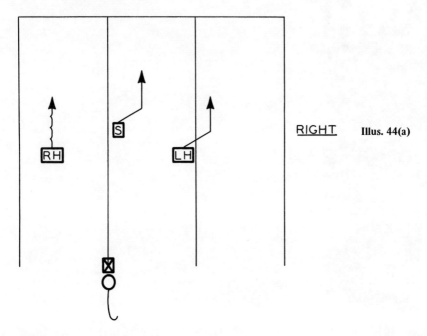

RIGHT   Illus. 44(a)

The purpose of this drill is to teach the deep backs the importance of playing the field.

INSTRUCTIONS

1. Station three deep backs on defense in the *center* of the field.

2. Use a center and passer on offense.

3. Have the passer fake one, two, or three times to make the defenders react, and then let him throw the ball.

4. Next move the defenders to the *right* hash mark and repeat the drill. After that station the defenders on the *left* hash mark, and repeat the drill.

5. See the three parts of Illustration 44.

Comment: This drill enables the defenders to increase the distance at which they can make interceptions and teaches them the value of playing the field.

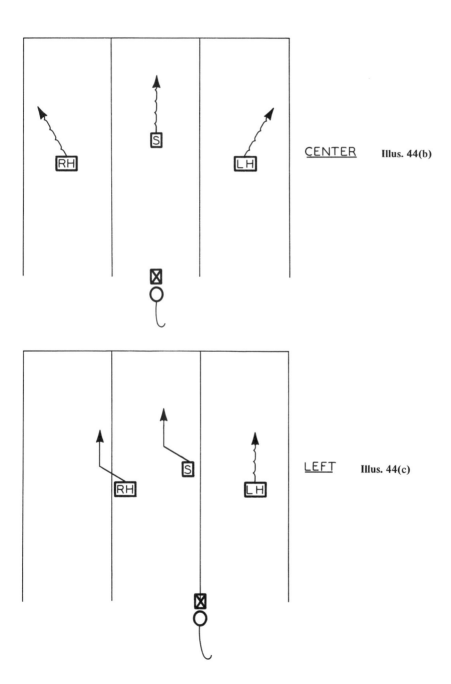

CENTER   Illus. 44(b)

LEFT   Illus. 44(c)

BULLDOG DRILL

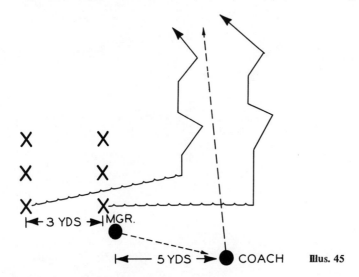

The purpose of this drill is to combine fighting for the ball and footwork. Good pass defenders fight for the ball like bulldogs.

INSTRUCTIONS

1. Line up two pass defenders 3 yards apart and facing you.

2. Let the inside defender be 5 yards from you.

3. Have a manager throw a ball to you as the defenders run laterally.

4. When you call "Go," have both defenders turn and run backward, following directional hand signals from you.

5. Throw the ball, and let the two defenders fight for it.

6. Have the defender who intercepts the ball go for the opposite goal line and the other defender try to tackle him.

7. If the defender goes all the way for a touchdown, award him 6 points.

8. See Illustration 45.

Comment: This is a drill that clearly indicates how aggressive a defender is, and the importance of footwork, position, and playing the ball.

INTERCEPT-AND-BLOCK DRILL

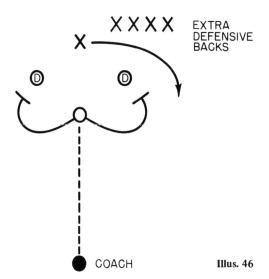

Illus. 46

The purpose of this drill is to provide practice for the players in meeting deflected balls and blocking back.

INSTRUCTIONS

1. Line up two men approximately 5 yards apart, facing you.

2. Have the front man move forward quickly toward you. As he does, you throw the ball high.

3. Let the front man tip the ball to the second man, the defensive player, who comes up under control and tries to intercept.

4. Ask the man who tipped the ball to turn around and block back, since he is the man closest to the receiver. Use two tall standing dummies for him to block.

5. See Illustration 46.

BLOCKING-BACK DRILL

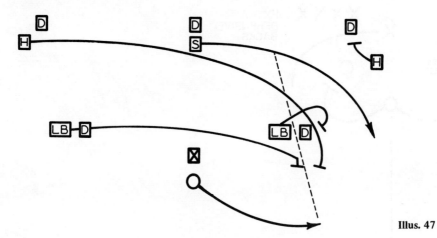

Illus. 47

The purpose of this drill is to enable players to practice blocking back on the intended receiver after an interception has been made.

INSTRUCTIONS

1. Place five comeback dummies in defensive positions. Locate them so that all areas are covered, with three dummies being deep and two short.

2. Station a center and quarterback on offense. If you have backfield personnel available, use them.

3. Have the quarterback use every type of backfield action possible: roll-out passes, bootleg passes, statue-of-liberty passes, play-action passes, run-pass plays, etc. (See Glossary.)

4. Have the defender nearest to the back making the interception block back on one of the comeback dummies (intended receiver). All other defenders should form a wall and turn upfield.

5. See Illustration 47.

LONG-INTERCEPTION DRILL

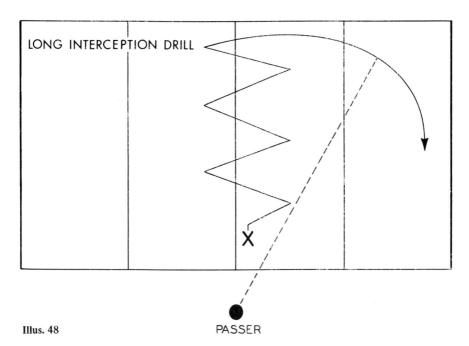

LONG INTERCEPTION DRILL

Illus. 48

PASSER

The purpose of this drill is to enable players to practice intercepting long forward passes.

INSTRUCTIONS

1. Station one, two, or three players on defense facing a passer.

2. Have the passer fake, to move the defensive man back and forth, and then let him throw the ball so that the defender must sprint to reach it. It is better to start with just one player on defense.

3. See Illustration 48.

Comment: Deep backs need training on intercepting long passes that are about 40 yards downfield. The flight of the ball on these long passes is different from the flight of a ball on short ones, because the nose is usually up, and the distance such a pass will travel can easily be misjudged. When a defender misjudges a pass of this type it usually results in a score. Usually the defender, unless he has been drilled on long passes, will play this type of pass too short.

LINE-DRIVE-INTERCEPTION DRILL

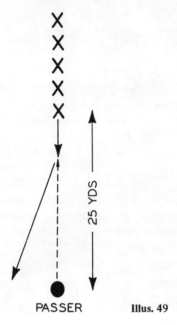

PASSER   Illus. 49

The purpose of this drill is to enable players to practice intercepting the football while coming into the ball with speed.

INSTRUCTIONS

1. Have the defenders line up 25 yards from the passer, usually a quarterback.

2. On a signal from the passer, have the lead player run at him.

3. Let the passer throw passes with plenty of velocity. He should vary the passes by throwing them high, wide, and low, but always like a bullet.

4. When the defender intercepts the ball, let him put it away and return it to a manager. Since this is a rapid-fire drill, someone is needed to feed footballs to the passer.

5. See Illustration 49.

Comment: This is a very good drill, and one that is needed if players are to practice line-drive interceptions that are often missed.

TIMING DRILL

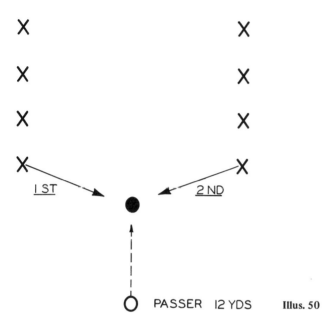

PASSER 12 YDS   Illus. 50

The purpose of this drill is to give the defensive players practice in coming from a distance at an angle to intercept the ball.

INSTRUCTIONS

1. One post man is needed in this drill; rotate him every six passes.

2. Station a passer 10 to 12 yards from the post player.

3. Station the pass defenders in lines 5 to 8 yards apart, and 2 to 3 yards deep.

4. As the passer raises his arm to throw, let the defenders start moving. Defenders in the two lines alternate running and trying to intercept the pass that is thrown to the post man.

5. See Illustration 50.

Comment: In this drill the passer is not trying to fool anyone.

BODY-POSITION DRILL

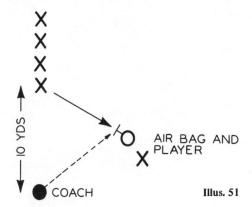

Illus. 51

The purpose of this drill is to enable players to practice intercepting the football, with emphasis on body position.

INSTRUCTIONS

1. Line up all the defensive backs in single file.

2. Use one player to hold an air dummy or shield about 6 or 7 yards from the first player in line.

3. Position yourself 10 yards from the player holding the air bag. Look at the bag and throw a pass directly toward it.

4. The defensive player, as soon as you look in that direction, starts running toward the shield and tries to intercept the ball.

5. As the player intercepts, let the man holding the dummy slam the bag into him.

6. Bear in mind that the coaching points for the defensive backs involved in this drill are: intercepting with two hands, being aggressive on going into the dummy, obtaining good body position on the interception (the defender does this by turning the side of his body into the bag), and putting the ball away after intercepting.

7. See Illustration 51.

TWIN CROSSING DRILL

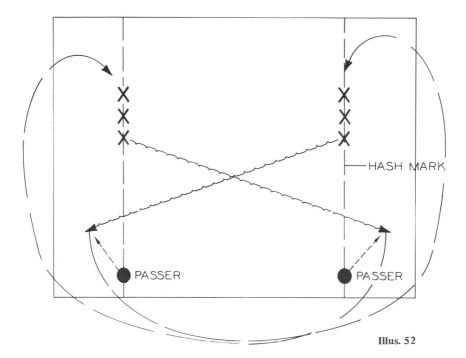

Illus. 52

The purpose of this drill is to give the players practice in intercepting the football while they are running forward, and in catching it at various angles.

INSTRUCTIONS

1. Have the defensive backs line up in two rows on their respective hash marks.

2. To avoid delays, arrange to have two passers and at least four footballs.

3. Have the line on the left break to the right and the line on the right break to the left.

4. Get each player to continue on around to the end of the other line after intercepting the ball.

5. See Illustration 52.

Comment: This is a rapid-fire interception drill that provides action for all the defensive backs when practice time is limited.

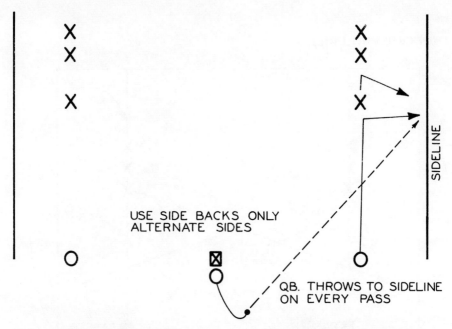

The purpose of this drill is to give players practice in intercepting sideline passes.

INSTRUCTIONS

1. Use only the side backs in this drill. Station them in their respective positions.

2. Have a center, two receivers and a quarterback on offense. As the quarterback retreats to make the pass, let the defensive back retreat with him, meanwhile watching both receiver and passer.

3. Have the quarterback throw a hard, deep pass near the sideline. If the defender has timed the pass properly, he will be *moving into* the ball as he makes his interception.

4. Be sure that the receiver and quarterback do not always do the same thing. Have the receiver run his sideline pattern at 6, then at 8, 10, 12, 14, 16, and 18 yards.

5. The drill is designed to train the defense in playing a sideline pass, and the quarterback should keep this in mind. The receiver is used only to help simulate game conditions.

6. Alternate sides in the drill. Have the quarterback employ only one side at a time.

7. See Illustration 53.

DOUBLE INTERCEPTION DRILL

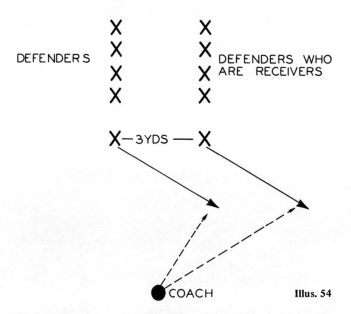

Illus. 54

The purpose of this drill is to provide practice for the defensive backs in intercepting a ball while they are running at an angle.

INSTRUCTIONS

1. Station the defensive backs and linebackers in two lines about 3 yards apart.

2. Designate one line as interceptors and another as receivers.

3. Position yourself 6 to 8 yards away.

4. As you raise your arm to throw the ball, let a player from each line break for the ball. If the ball is over-thrown, the men who are playing offense will try to catch it.

5. Alternate lines and directions so that the players get practice in meeting the ball from all angles.

6. See Illustration 54.

HEAVYWEIGHT-FOOTBALL DRILL

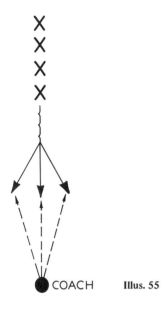

COACH   **Illus. 55**

The purpose of this drill is to help players develop the correct technique when they are intercepting. This is accomplished by means of a weighted football.

INSTRUCTIONS

1. Station all the pass defenders in one line on defense.

2. Arrange to have available several weighted footballs.

3. Locate a passer 10 yards from the front defender, or occupy that place yourself if you're feeling strong.

4. As you raise your arm to throw, let the first player in line move forward and try to intercept.

5. See Illustration 55.

Comment: A power-arm heavyweight football forces the defender to concentrate and focus his eyes on the ball when he is intercepting. If he doesn't, the ball will slip through his fingers. It also helps eliminate the "clash" of ball and hands that takes place on interceptions when the defender is moving forward. When a player is catching a weighted football, his hands must be "fluid," and he must accept the ball, not fight it. This is a good drill for backs who have "crowbar" fingers.

LOW-LINE-DRIVE DRILL

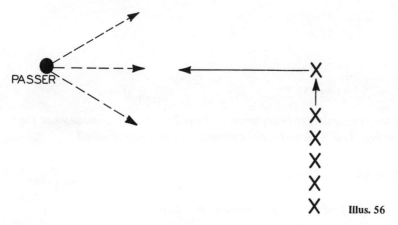

Illus. 56

The purpose of this drill is to enable players to practice intercepting low passes.

INSTRUCTIONS

1. Have the defensive players line up.

2. Station a passer 15 yards from the defenders, and have him throw low passes.

3. Have the pass defenders start running before the passer releases the ball.

4. See Illustration 56.

Comment: Line-drive passes are difficult to intercept, especially when they are low; that is, below the waist or knees. Many times the ball will hit the fingertips and still be missed, because the football sinks rapidly.

COFFIN-CORNER INTERCEPTION DRILL

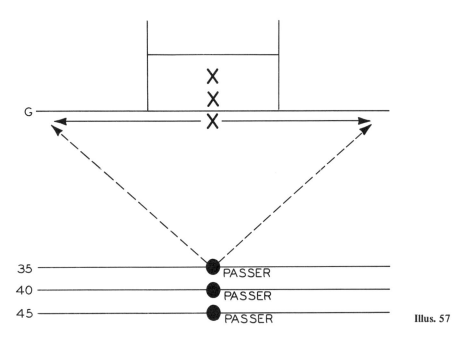

Illus. 57

The purpose of this drill is to help players develop the ability to cover more ground and intercept passes.

INSTRUCTIONS

1. Line the defenders up on the goal line in front of the goal post.

2. Locate the passer on the 35-yard line at midfield. Later move him back to the 40-yard line, and then to the 45-yard line.

3. Have the passer throw a high pass toward either coffin corner.

4. Let the defenders standing on the goal line try to intercept the ball, or, if they cannot catch it, bat it down.

5. Have them return the ball to you after intercepting.

6. See Illustration 57.

SHOTGUN DRILL

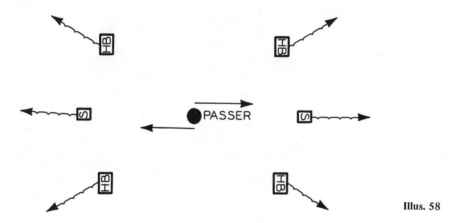

Illus. 58

The purpose of this drill is to work two defensive backfields when time is limited.

INSTRUCTIONS

1. Assemble two complete pass defense units, one on either side of the passer.

2. Have the passer alternate sides, throwing the ball first to one unit and then the other. Have him throw hard "shotgun" passes, as the backs retreat.

3. Let the passer try to throw the ball to open areas and force all the defenders to go for the ball.

4. Encourage the backs to lateral and in general interact with the other backs on their side when they are returning the interception.

5. See Illustration 58.

Comment: This is a fast-moving drill, good as an early-season or spring-practice drill, when a large number of defensive backs are available.

CHAPTER 6

PLAYING-THE-BALL DRILLS

In this chapter there are fifteen playing-the-ball drills, designed to help the defender in the following fundamental ways:

1. To improve his body balance and peripheral vision.
2. To improve his timing of interceptions.
3. To increase his interception distance.
4. To improve his judging of the ball in flight.
5. To improve his aggressiveness in separating the receiver from the ball.

One of the most important skills that the defender can acquire by means of these drills is the ability to keep his man covered and yet keep his vision clear so that he can spot other potential receivers. Most accomplished defenders have this ability.

Playing the ball is not something to be taken for granted. It can, however, be taught. Proper drilling can teach a man to play the ball while he is covering a receiver.

The majority of these playing-the-ball drills have been chosen to create situations that simulate game conditions. The drills in this chapter are interchangeable with drills for reaction, interception, and footwork.

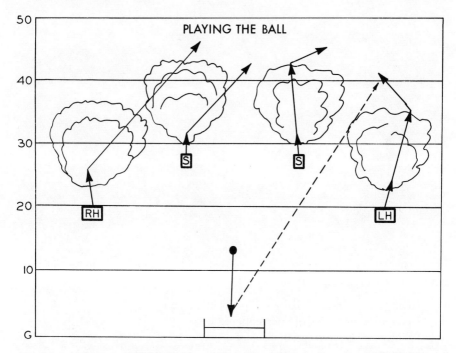

The purpose of this drill is to provide practice for the secondary in playing the ball both individually and as a group.

INSTRUCTIONS

1. Station the defensive backfield in their regular positions. Use as a football field the area between the 40-yard line and the goal line, and play the hash marks.

2. Let a quarterback or coach act as the passer. Have him drop back and throw downfield, throwing the ball so that it can be intercepted, but so that the defenders have to "stretch" for it. If the interception is too easy, they will loaf.

3. When the defender makes an interception, let him yell his call—"fire," "tiger," etc.—and then sprint for the opponent's end zone.

4. Insist that the defenders keep their eyes on the passer as they retreat.

5. Begin the drill by "playing the ball" with each individual, and then add the entire group.

6. Have the defender nearest the interceptor block back on an imaginary receiver. Get all defenders to cover on the ball once it is in the air, since all zones are out. Then have them form a picket and return the ball, just as they would on a punt return.

7. See Illustration 59.

INCREASING-INTERCEPTION-DISTANCE DRILL

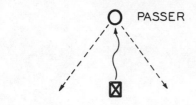

PASSER

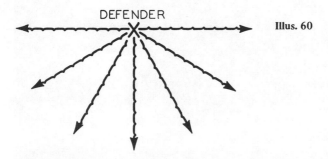

DEFENDER   Illus. 60

The purpose of this drill is to provide practice for the deep backs in playing the ball and to help them increase the distance they can cover after the football is in the air.

INSTRUCTIONS

1. Use both a center and a quarterback in this drill, if possible.

2. Station one defender approximately 8 to 10 yards deep.

3. As the quarterback retreats to pass, have the defender gain depth, using the footwork you wish him to use.

4. Let the passer throw the football 5 to 15 yards to either side of the defender, and also behind him, so that the defender can get the "break" on the ball and judge its flight.

5. Let the defender keep practicing until gradually he increases the distance he can cover and still reach the ball.

6. After the defender has increased his range, have the quarterback "pump" in one direction and throw in another.

7. See Illustration 60.

Comment: This drill gives the defender practice in telling the difference between a fake pass and the real thing. (Although passers like John Unitas can make anybody look bad!)

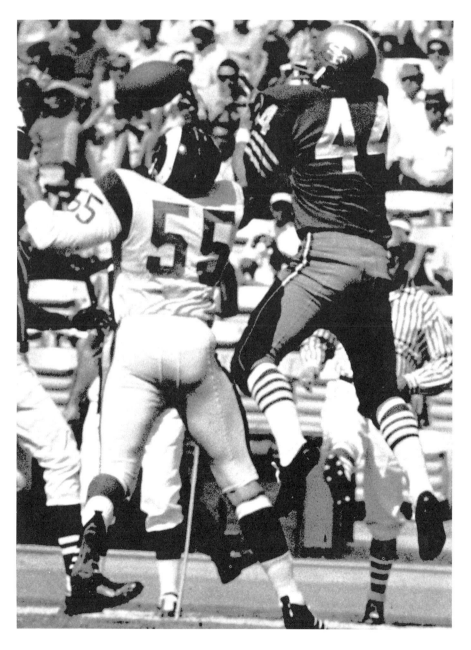

WATCHING-THE-PASSER DRILL

The purpose of this drill is to teach the defensive backs and linebackers to keep their eye on the passer and the football.

INSTRUCTIONS

1. Station five receivers downfield and have them run all around, some going short distances and some long.

2. Have each defender stick to his *zone* and play accordingly, totally disregarding the offensive players.

3. Let a coach or quarterback try to locate a receiver who is in the open and throw a pass to him. He must get the pass off in 4 seconds.

4. After the defensive players get accustomed to watching the football and not the receiver, add more receivers to the drill.

5. Have the defenders intercept the ball, form a picket, and bring it back.

6. Try a variation of this drill, which is to use 6 ends, three on each side of the center, and let them run any pattern they wish.

7. See the two parts of Illustration 61.

Comment: This drill is to be used when the defensive backs are concentrating too much on the receiver.

Illus. 61(a)

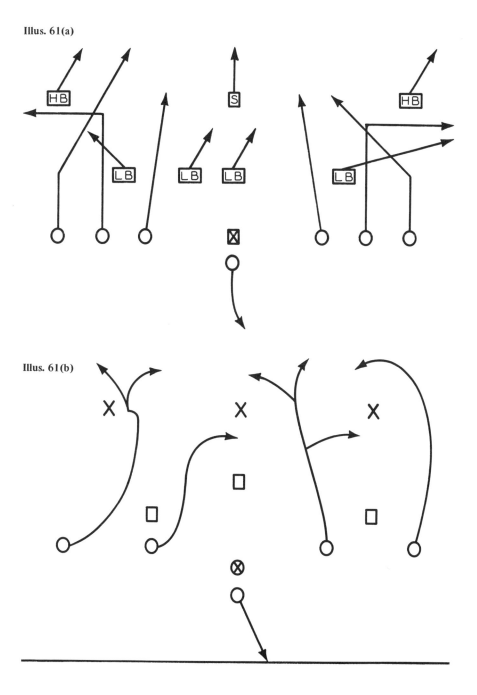

Illus. 61(b)

COVERING-ONE-THIRD-OF-THE-FIELD DRILL

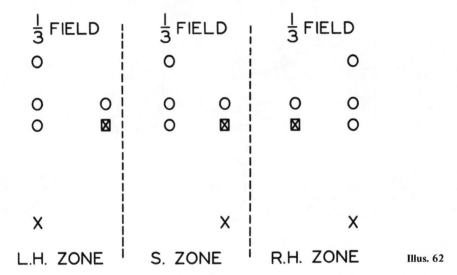

Illus. 62

The purpose of this drill is to give the defensive players certain zones to cover and see how many passes they can break up.

INSTRUCTIONS

1. Station three lines of receivers on offense. Have a center and a passer for each group.

2. Station your left halfback, safety man, and right halfback in their respective zones.

3. The pass receivers may use any type of maneuver they want to get into the open, but they cannot run out of their specified one-third area to catch a pass.

4. See Illustration 62.

Comment: This drill is a good one for both the offensive ends and all the defenders.

BAD-PASS DRILL

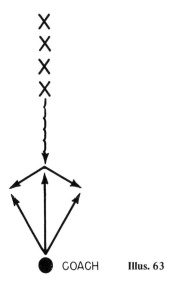

COACH   **Illus. 63**

The purpose of this drill is to give the pass defenders practice in catching a badly thrown pass.

INSTRUCTIONS

1. Station the defensive backs in line, one behind the other.

2. On a signal from you, let the first back in line come forward.

3. Throw the football in all sorts of ways: high, low, fast, slow, wide, or wobbling.

4. Have the defender run forward and try to catch the ball, regardless of where it is thrown. He must maintain balance regardless of his speed.

5. Start the drill at half speed, so that the players are under control at the beginning, and gradually build up to top speed.

6. Have a manager standing by to feed balls to you.

7. Tell the defensive backs not to start running until you have the ball in your possession; if they start before that, they get too close.

8. See Illustration 63.

ELASTIC DRILL

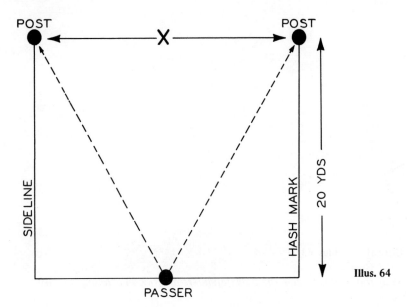

Illus. 64

The purpose of this drill is to teach the halfback how to cover his one-third of the field.

INSTRUCTIONS

1. Place one post man on the sideline and one on the hash mark. Station these players 20 yards downfield from a passer.

2. Station one defensive halfback midway between the post men.

3. Have the passer try to throw to either one of the post men. Let the defender try to knock the ball down or intercept it. If the defender is doing a good job, he will break up 7 out of 10 passes.

4. Unless you happen to have a strong passing arm, it is better to use a reserve quarterback, Junior Varsity quarterback, or freshman quarterback as the passer. The defender gets more out of the drill when there is a strong passer and the practice is beneficial to the quarterback also.

5. See Illustration 64.

BUST-IT DRILL

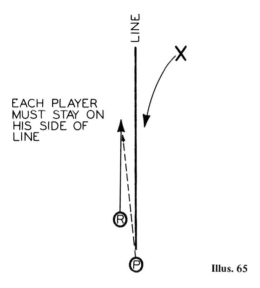

Illus. 65

The purpose of this drill is to teach the defender to ignore the receiver and play the ball.

INSTRUCTIONS

1. Station a passer and a defender 15 yards apart.

2. Use an end as receiver. At the command of the passer, have the end go downfield.

3. Let the passer throw to the end and the defender try to intercept or break up the play.

4. Make all three players stay within the zone defined by three 5-yard markers. Each player should stay on his own side of the middle chalk line.

5. Have the defender ignore the receiver and play the ball. When, as occasionally happens, the receiver crosses the line, the defender should "bust in" and go for the football.

6. See Illustration 65.

Comment: We call this our "bust-it" drill because the defender, if he is aggressive, will bust in and try to intercept.

BACKBOARD DRILL

The purpose of this drill is to provide practice for the pass defenders in fighting for the ball and playing it at its highest point.

INSTRUCTIONS

1. Use a fence or wall as a backboard.

2. Line up players in pairs.

3. Throw the football against the wall and let two players at a time go up in the air and fight for possession of it.

4. Stress going up with two hands, using hips and whole body to attain the best possible position, and timing of the jump so that the player reaches the ball at its highest elevation.

SQUARE JUMPING DRILL

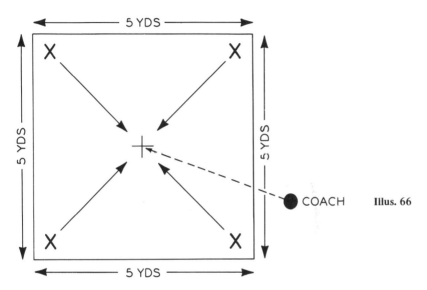

Illus. 66

The purpose of this drill is to help the players practice getting up in the air and playing a football at its highest point.

INSTRUCTIONS

1. Station one player in each corner of a 5-yard square.

2. Throw a football high in the air in the center of the square, so that no player has an advantage.

3. To begin with, forbid the players to use their hands to get the ball. Each man must learn to use his *body* like a basketball player taking a rebound. This helps him to time the jump correctly.

4. After players have practiced using their bodies and have become accustomed to contact, allow them to use their hands and jump high to intercept the ball.

5. See Illustration 66.

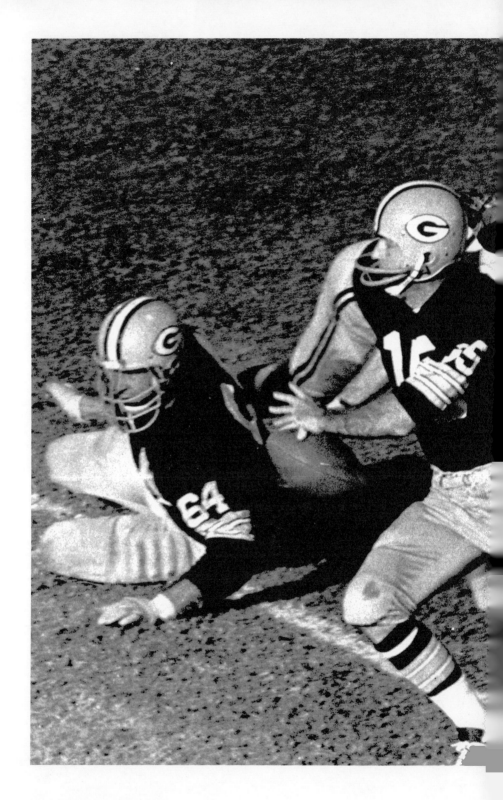

JUMPING DRILL

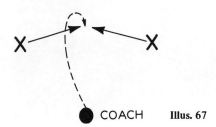

COACH   Illus. 67

The purpose of this drill is to enable players to practice jumping and the use of the body in going up in the air after the football.

INSTRUCTIONS

1.   Have two players stand facing each other, just as though they were getting ready for the center jump in basketball.

2.   Stand next to the players and toss the ball up between them.

3.   Have the defenders time their jumps so that they reach the ball at its highest point. Insist that they play the ball with *both* hands.

4.   Do *not* allow the players, when they are playing the ball, to use their hands on the opponent. If they develop good habits in jumping, there is little chance that they will cause a penalty for interference with a pass receiver when they are in an actual game.

5.   See Illustration 67.

INSIDE-RECOVERY DRILL

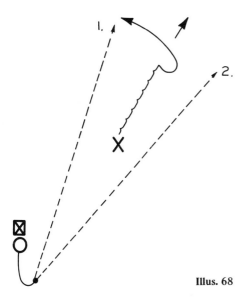

Illus. 68

The purpose of this drill is to enable defensive players to work on the shoulder dip so that a man learns how to recover a ball thrown to his inside.

INSTRUCTIONS

1. Use one defender at a time. Have him assume his stance.

2. Station a passer and center 8 yards from the defender. When the ball is snapped from the center, let the defender start backward.

3. Have the passer throw beyond the defender, mainly to his inside.

4. To keep the defender alert for both inside *and* outside passes, let the passer occasionally throw to the outside.

5. Insist that the defender make a quick recovery by dipping his inside shoulder and making a quick turn away from the ball momentarily, to gain both depth and speed.

6. Have the defender turn his head quickly to refocus his eyes on the football and sprint to a position to intercept the ball (or cover the receiver, if there is one).

7. Have the defender return the football by sprinting back to the passer.

8. See Illustration 68.

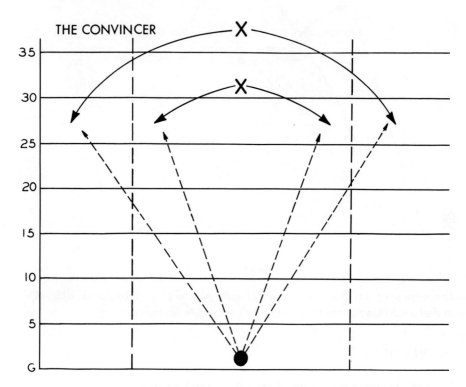

The purpose of this drill is to convince the pass defender of the great distance he can cover while the ball is in the air.

INSTRUCTIONS

1. Start the drill with a defender stationed 30 yards from a passer.

2. Have the passer throw the ball to an imaginary receiver in the area.

3. Let the defender assume his stance and watch the long-arm action of the passer. Have him intercept the ball at its highest point and run the ball back to the passer.

4. After the defender has the range, move the passer 10 yards deeper, and continue the process, moving the passer away as far as possible.

5. Have the defender yell "Fire!" as he intercepts the pass.

6. See Illustration 69.

TIMING-THE-CUT DRILL   Illus. 70

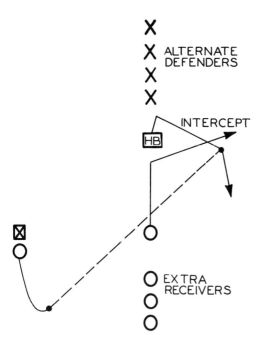

The purpose of this drill is to give the defender practice in cutting in front of a receiver to intercept a forward pass.

INSTRUCTIONS

1. Station all the deep backs on defense, but use only one defender at a time.

2. Station a receiver with a center and quarterback on offense.

3. Limit the receiver to sideline patterns only in this drill.

4. Have the passer throw outs to a receiver and try to complete them. Tell the passer not to favor the defender, but make him "earn" his interceptions.

5. Let the defender watch both the receiver and the passer. Have him time his cut so that he can intercept the ball while he is moving forward.

6. Stay with this drill until the defender gets the "feeling" of his break for the ball.

7. See Illustration 70.

Comment: This is a fine drill, and one that the cornerbacks need.

LOB DRILL

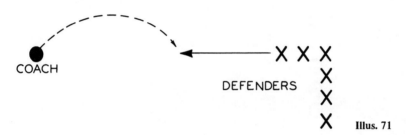

COACH

DEFENDERS

Illus. 71

The purpose of this drill is to enable the players to practice intercepting a ball that has been lobbed high in the air.

INSTRUCTIONS

1. Line up defensive players.

2. Station yourself about 20 to 35 yards away, and pass to a certain spot well in front of the first man in line.

3. Have the defenders start running forward before you release the ball; this makes the drill more difficult.

4. Throw high and long on every pass.

5. Have the defenders time their jumps so that they intercept the ball at its highest point, recover quickly, and sprint to you with the football.

6. See Illustration 71.

Comment: Many times defenders misjudge a football that has been arched to them. This is a matter of timing, and to iron out this difficulty takes practice.

SPEED DRILL

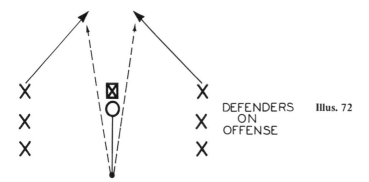

Illus. 72

DEFENDERS ON OFFENSE

The purpose of this drill is to provide a warm-up for the defensive backs, while at the same time allowing them to handle the ball as much as possible in a short interval.

INSTRUCTIONS

1. Have all the defenders form two lines on each side of the passer. Use a re-serve quarterback if possible in this drill, with a center.

2. As quickly as the quarterback can throw, have the defenders release for a pass.

3. Have the quarterback throw only short passes, and let each defender place the ball on the ground next to the center as he returns.

4. Use plenty of footballs.

5. See Illustration 72.

Comment: It is a rapid-fire drill, and it is amazing how many passes each defender can catch and how much running takes place within 2 or 3 minutes. This is also an excellent drill for offensive ends.

HALF-CIRCLE DRILL

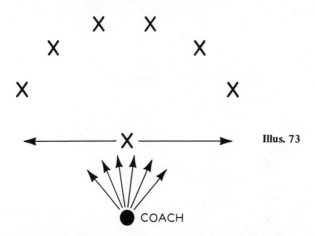

Illus. 73

The purpose of this drill is to teach players to read the passer's eyes. It is also a fine drill to improve footwork and agility.

INSTRUCTIONS

1. Arrange six players in a half circle. Station one player three yards out in front of the circle.

2. Have the player who is out in front assume a proper defensive stance, with his feet moving in place. He must focus his eyes on you.

3. You, acting as a passer, look at one of the players in the half circle and throw the football toward him.

4. The defensive player should read your eyes first, and then the ball. Wherever you look, the player must try to align himself between the player you are looking at and you, before you throw the ball.

5. The player who receives the ball quickly throws it back to you.

6. All the fundamentals of secondary defense are involved in this drill: stance, footwork, agility, quickness, and reading the passer's eyes.

7. See Illustration 73.

CHAPTER 7

DEFLECTION DRILLS

Not very long ago pass defenders did *not* practice reacting to deflected passes. When a tipped ball was intercepted it was considered just a lucky break. This is no longer correct, because deflection drills represent a true picture of game conditions. *Practice the way you intend to play* and you cannot go wrong.

At first just one drill was employed, and that lone drill was used by almost every coach who wanted a deflection drill for his linebackers and secondary men.

At present there are so many good deflection drills that they merit a separate chapter. They deserve a classification of their own because they are entirely different from the other defensive drills. Usually these drills are mixed in with other secondary drills, and labeled deflection drill 1, deflection drill 2, etc. Here we have a separate chapter devoted to them, so that the reader can readily locate a drill to his liking.

In the case of a deflected pass, reaction is everything. This reaction is something that must be practiced because it is *not* a natural type of movement. Not only the deep backs, but also the linebackers need this type of training so that they can react correctly when there is a deflected pass, even when they least expect it. In some years the linebackers intercept more deflected passes than the deep backs.

In almost every football game, regardless of the level of competition, the defense will have several opportunities to "pick off" a deflected ball. Statistics indicate that in any given year approximately 6 of a team's interceptions result from deflected passes.

Keep an accurate record of the number of balls deflected by each defensive player, and also a record of the passes he intercepts that were originally tipped by someone. This will indicate the value of devoting some practice time to the playing of deflected forward passes.

OPPOSITE-DIRECTION DRILL

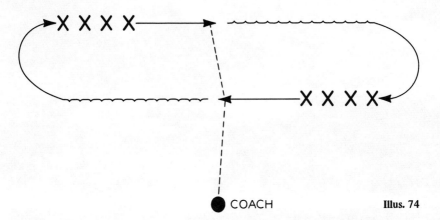

COACH   Illus. 74

The purpose of this drill is to give the players practice in intercepting deflected passes coming from the opposite direction.

INSTRUCTIONS

1. Line up in single file the players who are to do the deflecting. They should be located 15 yards from you and should run across the field.

2. Line up the defenders who are to intercept the deflected balls 5 to 8 yards deeper. These players should run, under control, in the opposite direction and will become deflectors in the next line.

3. Throw a hard pass to the first line of players. Have them try to deflect it to the second line of players.

4. See Illustration 74.

Comment: This is one of the variations in the deflected-ball drill series.

GOING-AWAY DRILL

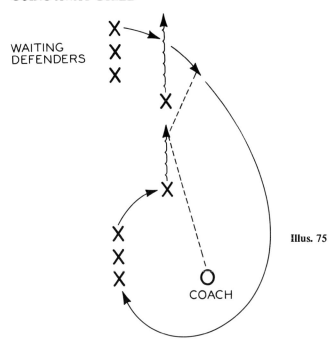

WAITING
DEFENDERS

COACH

Illus. 75

The purpose of this drill is to give the players practice in intercepting a batted ball while going away from it.

INSTRUCTIONS

1. Station two lines of players in single file, one line to deflect and one to intercept.

2. If you are to do the passing, position yourself as shown in Illustration 75.

3. As you retreat, have both lines start going backward. Throw the ball on a line to the front man in the line nearest you, who attempts to bat the ball to the front man in the second line. Have players alternate lines, so that each man has a chance to become both a deflector and an interceptor.

4. Make sure that the defender keeps a distance of at least 5 yards from the player who is deflecting the football. In addition, see to it that he continues to run backward until the ball leaves your hand.

5. See Illustration 75.

Comment: Many times a deflected ball falls just short of the defender's fingertips because he was backing up, took that *extra* step, and could not adjust. This drill helps him lick that problem.

LATERAL-DEFLECTION DRILL

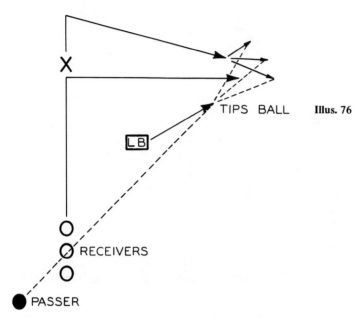

Illus. 76

The purpose of this drill is to give defensive players practice in covering a receiver who is running a specific pattern and yet keeping the defenders alert for a tipped ball.

INSTRUCTIONS

1.   Station a corner man and a linebacker on defense. Locate several receivers and a passer on offense.

2.   Have the pass receiver run "outs" only. Let the defender try to stay with the receiver and cover him.

3.   Tell the linebacker to get depth and when possible deflect the football. If the pass is underthrown, let the linebacker intercept it.

4.   See Illustration 76.

Comment: Corner men who are in a good position on the receiver are often focusing too much attention on him and fail to see the football in flight. This drill helps teach them to do both things at once.

HIGH-DEFLECTION DRILL

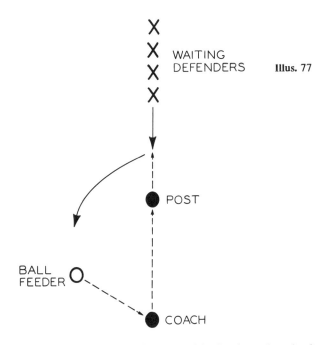

Illus. 77

The purpose of this drill is to enable the three deep backs and the linebackers to practice playing high deflected balls.

INSTRUCTIONS

1. Line up all the defensive backs in single file. If there are too many defenders, divide the group into two units so that everyone is busy.

2. Position yourself (or a passer) 15 to 20 yards from the front defender.

3. Station a player to act as a post man to deflect the passes. His job is to tip the ball so that it has elevation.

4. Tell the front defender not to start forward until you pass the football. He must come up under control (see Glossary).

5. Have the defender, using *two* hands, try to intercept the ball at its highest point. Also have him grab the ball out in front of him, with arms extended forward, and then put it away under his arm. Have him always return the ball to you or to a manager.

6. See Illustration 77.

Deflection drills 123

ANGLE-DEFLECTION DRILL

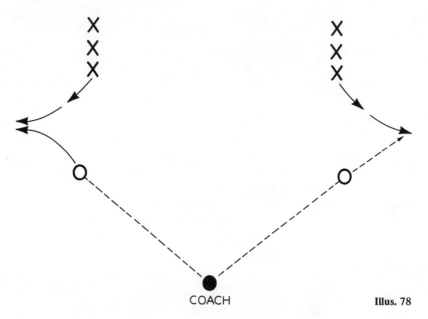

Illus. 78

The purpose of this drill is to provide practice for the pass defenders in reacting to deflected balls while running at an angle.

INSTRUCTIONS

1. Line up the defenders, single file, in two lines, 15 yards from you, or from the passer.

2. Position two players to act as deflectors. (There is a good bit of skill involved in this; the men in these spots have a lot to do with making the drill effective.)

3. Tell the defender not to start forward until you raise your arm to throw. He must always be approximately 5 yards from the deflector.

4. See to it that the deep defenders are always running at an angle when they are running forward, which simulates game conditions, because in a game they seldom come straight forward to break up a pass. If the deflector bats the ball, they have to react at an angle when they intercept.

5. See Illustration 78.

Comment: This is a good fast-moving drill and the players like it. Have plenty of footballs and someone to help you when the defender returns the interception.

PURE-REACTION DRILL

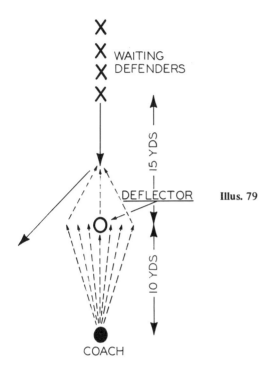

Illus. 79

The purpose of this drill is to test the defenders' reactions against all types of passes.

INSTRUCTIONS

1. Line up the pass defenders in single file. Place a player who is adept at setting up deflections 15 yards in front of the first defender.

2. Position yourself or a reserve quarterback 10 yards from the deflector. Throw every type of forward pass possible: high, low, left, right, fast, slow, wobbly, etc. This drill calls for all the coaching points of the previous drills.

3. Let the deflector tip these erratic balls as best he can toward the defender, who is running forward.

4. Keep score and see who can intercept three passes first. This should be a fast-moving drill. You will need a manager to assist you.

5. See Illustration 79.

Comment: We call this our "pure reaction" drill because neither the defender nor the deflector know where the pass will be.

Deflection drills 125

HOOK-PASS DRILL

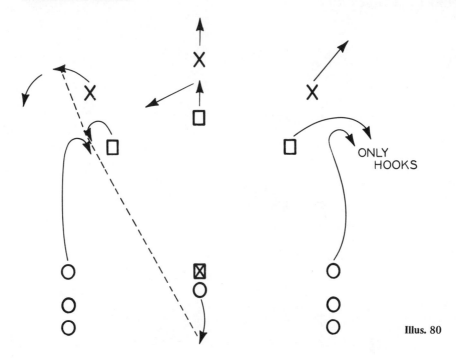

Illus. 80

The purpose of this drill is to give deep pass defenders and linebackers practice in playing a deflected pass.

INSTRUCTIONS

1. Place three linebackers on defense, with three pass defenders.

2. Station two receivers, a center, and yourself on offense. The receivers are limited in what they can run, since this is a hook drill.

3. Have the linebackers try to get good position on the receivers. When they do, have them tip the ball, in any direction they can, so that the pass defenders must be alert and ready to react.

4. Throw hard, high passes to the receivers. Complete passes to the ends. Occasionally, just to keep the defenders on their toes, throw a pass right at one of them.

5. When the receiver is in the open, he may catch the ball and put it away or deflect it in any direction.

6. See Illustration 80.

DOUBLE DEFLECTION DRILL

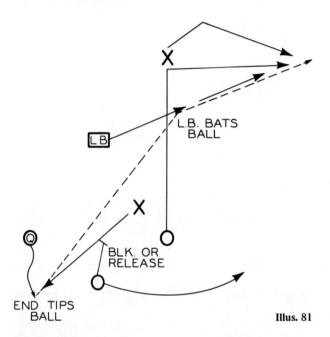

Illus. 81

The object of this drill is to give the defender practice in reacting to a ball that has been deflected twice.

INSTRUCTIONS

1. Place on defense an end, a linebacker, and a defensive back. Locate on offense a receiver, a halfback, and a quarterback.

2. Have the defensive end rush the passer on every play and come in with hands high. (This is excellent practice for the defensive end and the passer.)

3. Tell the halfback to either block the defensive end or release for a pass, depending on the call in the huddle. For the most part the halfback should just fake a block and allow the end to come in. Occasionally let him set strong and belt the end, just to keep him honest.

4.   Let the quarterback try to complete to his receiver a pass that has been de-
     cided on in the huddle. Occasionally let him throw line drives so that the
     defensive end is able to tip the ball just enough to take off the spiral. When
     this happens the linebacker, if he can, should also deflect the pass, so that the
     defender can intercept a ball that has been touched twice.

5.   Have the receiver run outs, crosses, and hooks.

6.   See Illustration 81.

Comment: This is a variation of the other drills, to be used as a change in practice
routine. Since this is a timing drill, players can learn a lot from every play, whether
the ball is tipped once, twice, or not at all.

FORWARD DEFLECTION DRILL

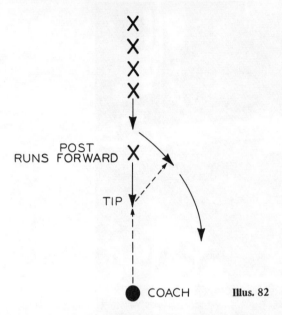

POST
RUNS FORWARD

TIP

COACH   Illus. 82

The purpose of this drill is again to provide the secondary with vital practice in playing a deflected football.

INSTRUCTIONS

1. Align players the same way as in the High Deflection Drill, with the defenders in single file and a post man 10 yards ahead.

2. If you act as passer yourself, station yourself 10 yards from the deflector.

3. In this drill, unlike the previous drill in which the post man was stationary, have the post man come running forward as you raise your arm to throw.

4. Let the defender also start forward, but keep a distance of 5 yards between himself and the moving post man.

5. Have the post man deflect the forward pass and the defender try to react so that he can intercept.

6. Let the ball be deflected high, low, wide, etc.

7. See Illustration 82.

Comment: This is a good variation of the other drills, in that, when a man is running forward and trying to tip the ball, he usually puts a different spin on it each time, and that is what you are after.

BALL-POSSESSION DRILL

The purpose of this drill is to teach the pass defenders the fundamentals of fighting for a deflected ball.

INSTRUCTIONS

1. Use this drill after you have used the forward and opposite-direction drills, to show the pass defenders what they have learned from the previous drills.

2. Station the pass defenders in two lines, facing you (or the passer).

3. Station a deflector 10 yards from you, and let him try to tip the ball when you pass it.

4. Have two players run forward and try to intercept the tipped ball.

5. To begin with, have the deflector try to tip the ball to either one man or the other.

6. After awhile, tell the deflector to tip it in such a way that it's anybody's ball, and tell the two pass defenders to fight for it.

7. See the two parts of Illustration 83.

Comment: This drill teaches the players to be ready for a deflected pass, and to use their whole body—hips, arms, and both hands—to fight for the batted football. Since this drill simulates what takes place in a game when the ball is being batted around, it is a good drill. More drills of this type are needed.

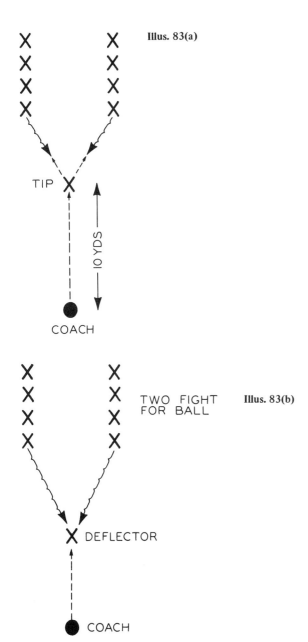

DUMMY DEFLECTION DRILL

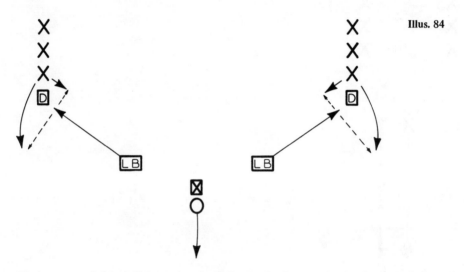

The purpose of this drill is to give the defensive backs practice in playing a deflected ball.

INSTRUCTIONS

1. Station two lines of defensive backs behind two standing dummies in the hook zone. Use two linebackers on defense.

2. Place a center and a reserve quarterback on offense; let them be approximately 10 yards in front of the dummies.

3. As the passer fades back to throw, let the linebackers go to the hook zones which are their respective responsibilities.

4. Have the quarterback throw a hard, high pass and the linebacker tip the ball. Tell the defensive back to try to intercept the ball at its highest point.

5. Point out that the dummies represent offensive ends, and are supposed to act as obstacles in the paths of the defenders as they go after the ball.

6. See Illustration 84.

BLOCK-VARIATION DRILL

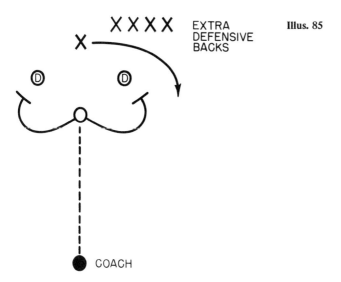

Illus. 85

The purpose of this drill is to give the players practice in meeting deflected balls and blocking back.

INSTRUCTIONS

1. Line up two men approximately 5 yards apart, facing you.

2. Have the front man move forward quickly toward you. As he does, you throw the ball high.

3. Let the front man tip the ball to the second man, the defensive player, who comes up under control and tries to intercept.

4. Ask the man who tipped the ball to turn around and block back, since he is the man closest to the receiver. Use two tall standing dummies for him to block.

5. See Illustration 85.

END-LINEBACKER DEFLECTION DRILL

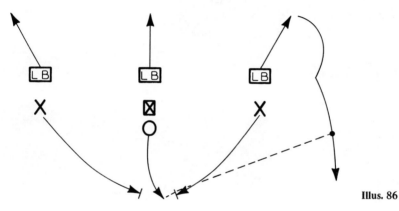

Illus. 86

The purpose of this drill is to give both the defensive ends and the linebackers practice in playing a batted ball.

INSTRUCTIONS

1. Station three linebackers and two defensive ends on defense.

2. Use a reserve quarterback with a center on offense.

3. As soon as the quarterback sets up to pass, have the ends rush the quarterback with arms extended and try to tip the football so that the linebackers get a chance to play the batted ball.

4. See Illustration 86.

Comment: This drill duplicates the relationship the linebackers have to the defensive backs in a game, and thus it is a drill the linebackers need. The defensive ends also receive valuable training in getting off with the ball, rushing the passer from outside, and making him throw as though he were "standing in a well."

LINEBACKER AND SECONDARY DRILL

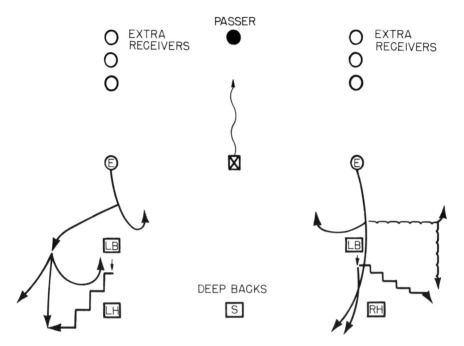

The purpose of this drill is to enable the deep backs, while they are in their normal defense positions, to practice handling tipped balls.

INSTRUCTIONS

1. Station three or four deep defenders in their regular positions.

2. Locate two or three linebackers in their regular positions.

3. Station a center and quarterback on offense. As the quarterback retreats and sets up to pass, let the linebackers retreat to their zones.

4. Have the passer throw high line drives at the linebackers, who try to either tip the ball or intercept it.

5. After interceptions, have everyone form a picket and return the ball.

6. See Illustration 87.

138 Deflection drills

CHAPTER 8

TACKLING DRILLS

No deep back ever has achieved greatness unless he has combined tackling ability with covering ability. *Tackling is the backbone of defense.* It is the "blood and guts" of defensive team play.

Courage is no substitute for technique. *No matter how much courage a player has, he must be taught the proper fundamentals of tackling.* The best way to start to teach tackling is to begin on a dummy, so that a player can gain confidence. However, some players are "soft tacklers," and although they may improve somewhat as time goes by, they never develop into solid tacklers.

It requires real fortitude to play on the defensive platoon. The offensive personnel get all the publicity and glamor. Most football devotees know how many passes each receiver has caught, the rushing average of the backs, and how many touchdowns So-and-so has scored. However, everyone appreciates a good tackler, and players, fans, and coaches all have the highest respect for these hitters.

This chapter gives 15 tackling drills for the deep backs. Many other tackling drills were omitted because we felt that only the choice drills should be included. All the following drills have been tried, tested, and proved.

FORM TACKLING DRILL

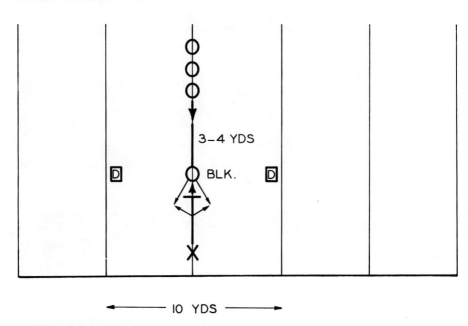

The purpose of this drill is to teach, at half-speed, the basic fundamentals of tackling.

INSTRUCTIONS

1. Separate the defensive backs into offense and defense. If there are not enough players, add the linebackers.

2. Have one blocker to go with each ball carrier. Have him block at least three yards in front of the runner.

3. Let the defender try to ward off the blocker and make the tackle.

4. Let the runner next become a blocker and the blocker a runner. Give every player 3 turns, and don't forget that this is a drill for the secondary.

5. Be sure to limit the area by using yard-line markers or dummies; otherwise the defenders will not gain much from the drill.

6. To avoid confusion, have each blocker and runner decide which direction he is to try to block and run. Occasionally have the runner try to go right through the tackler without any help from the blocker.

7. Tell the defender to run forward to meet the blocker and try to push him down. The defender should *not* be *waiting* for the blocker and runner to come to him.

8. See Illustration 88.

Comment: This is a drill to teach form in tackling. It also incorporates practice in the meeting of a blocker, and the defensive backs usually need plenty of this.

THREE-BAG TACKLING DRILL

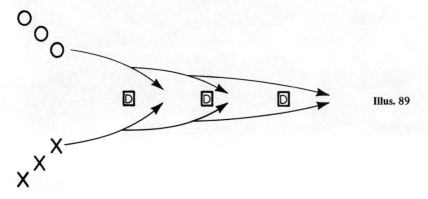

Illus. 89

The purpose of this drill is to provide the deep backs with practice in tackling, with some variations.

INSTRUCTIONS

1. Place three standing dummies in a straight line. Space the dummies so that there's room enough for a ball carrier to run between them.

2. Line up the pass defenders opposite the ball carriers.

3. Let a runner go through any hole, at any speed he desires. Have the tackler approach under control and keep position on the runner.

4. After each man has had three tackles, switch the drill to the other side, so that the tacklers may get practice using the other shoulder.

5. See Illustration 89.

PLAYING-THE-BLOCKER DRILL

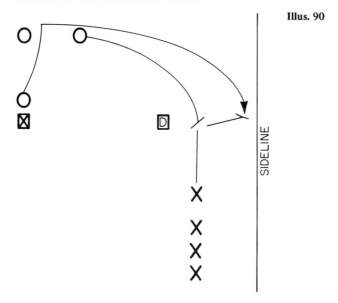

Illus. 90

The purpose of this drill is to train the deep backs to play a blocker on a sweep and tackle the runner, or knock him out of bounds.

INSTRUCTIONS

1. Use a tall stand-up dummy 12 yards from the sideline. All plays are to go around this bag.

2. Let the offense consist of a center, quarterback, fullback, and halfback. Let the defense consist only of the cornermen.

3. Have the runner follow his halfback, who tries to block the defender any way he can. Every time the runner gets past the tackler, let it count 6 points for the offense; every time he is stopped, let it count 6 points for the defense.

4. Tell the tackler not to let the blocker get to his legs, but to use his hands and push the blocker down. The tackler should use the sideline and attempt to force the blocker outside.

5. Have the defender take his proper stance and alignment before each play, otherwise defenders start cheating, i.e., edging closer to the line of scrimmage.

6. See Illustration 90.

MASS TACKLING DRILL

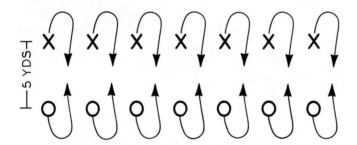

Illus. 91

The purpose of this drill is to give players mass tackling practice, save time, and improve organization, especially when there is a limited coaching staff.

INSTRUCTIONS

1. Arrange all the defensive halfbacks in two lines, 5 yards apart.

2. Identify one line as offense and one as defense. Have the lines stand so that they are back to back.

3. Have one line pivot on the right foot, the other line on the left foot.

4. Let the men in the offensive line each carry a football and run hard into the tackler opposite him.

5. Let each man in the defensive line assume a low, balanced football position and make the tackle.

6. You and the other coaches should concentrate on the players that need instructions in tackling.

7. See Illustration 91.

Comment: This is a good tackling drill, in which everyone can get a maximum amount of practice in a minimum amount of time.

GOAL-LINE TACKLING DRILL

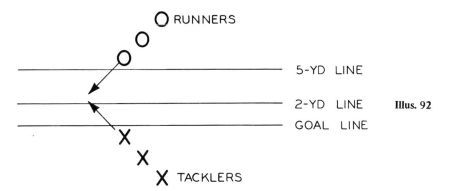

The purpose of this drill is to practice tackling under competitive conditions while trying to prevent a score.

INSTRUCTIONS

1. Station the offensive backs on the 5-yard line, their object being to reach the end zone and score a touchdown.

2. Locate the tacklers on the 2-yard line. As each runner starts forward, let a tackler move to meet him at an angle.

3. After several plays, reverse the angle so that the tacklers can use the other shoulder.

4. See Illustration 92.

Comment: This is angle tackling, and puts the pressure on the defensive halfback.

KEYING AND SUPPORTING DRILL

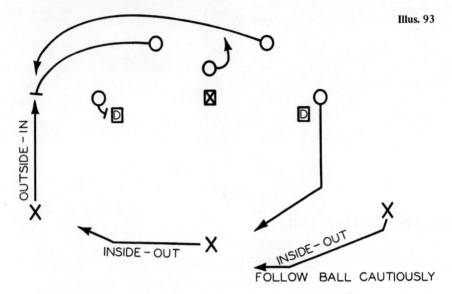

Illus. 93

The purpose of this drill is to give the secondary practice in keying and supporting on an end run.

INSTRUCTIONS

1. Arrange two units, one on offense and one on defense. Let the offense consist of a quarterback, center, and at least two backs. (Since the offense takes a beating in this drill, use some players from the Junior Varsity.)

2. Station three or four defenders in the secondary.

3. Locate two standing dummies in the spots normally occupied by the defensive ends.

4. Have the offense run all wide plays to both sides. The defense does not know which side they will run until the snap.

5. When you use offensive ends, ask them to block the dummies or occasionally release downfield for a running pass. Tell the ends to fake a block before releasing.

6. Have all the blockers and the ball carriers detour around the dummies to keep the ideal alignment and make the drill simulate game conditions.

7. After one defensive unit has had enough work, substitute another. See to it that each player gets in at least three solid tackles.

8. See Illustration 93.

SUPPORTING-UP-THE-GUT DRILL

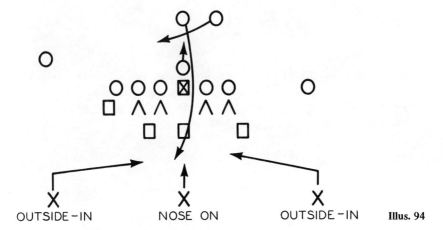

OUTSIDE-IN   NOSE ON   OUTSIDE-IN   **Illus. 94**

The purpose of this drill is to give the secondary practice in supporting the line when a running play comes up the middle.

INSTRUCTIONS

1. Arrange an offensive and a defensive unit.

2. Use a quarterback, center, and at least two backs on offense.

3. Station a complete secondary on defense. You may add linebackers as the drill progresses. However, if you use them with defensive linemen, they remain inactive.

4. See Illustration 94.

Comment: This drill is similar to the previous one. Defensive halfbacks have a tendency to over-run on plays up the middle; therefore this drill helps them to learn the proper angle for support.

CIRCLE DRILL

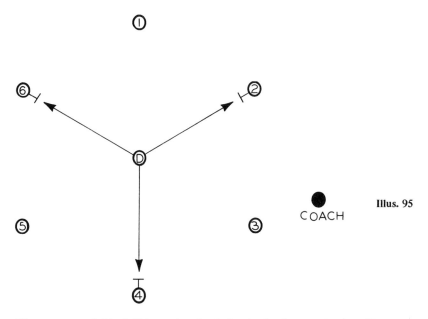

Illus. 95

The purpose of this drill is to give the defensive backs practice in taking on a blocker.

INSTRUCTIONS

1. Arrange six players in a circle, with one defender in the center. Each back in the circle is numbered, and as you call a number, that player tries to block the defender.

2. The player in the center of the circle must meet the block with a good base, protect himself with his hands or forearms, and be alert for a blocker from any direction.

3. Do not allow the blocker to hit the defensive player from the rear.

4. Be sure to allow enough time between blocks for the man in the middle to recover and get on his guard.

5. See Illustration 95.

Comment: The defensive backs usually get plenty of practice tackling, but often they don't know the fundamentals of meeting a blocker. It is hard to practice both at the same time. Therefore this drill is essential for all defenders. It is also especially good for the corner men.

THREE-ON-THREE REVERSE TACKLING DRILL

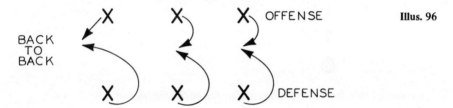

Illus. 96

The purpose of this drill is to teach players proper position of the tackler on the runner.

INSTRUCTIONS

1. Station the defenders in two rows, back to back and 5 yards apart. Designate one row as the offense and the other as the defense.

2. When you give a signal, let both reverse positions. Have each runner try to evade the tackler opposite him.

3. Next station the defender in a reverse position, with the offensive player already facing forward and ready to move forward.

4. Stress position of head, arms, and feet, and all basic fundamentals of tackling.

5. See Illustration 96.

Comment: This drill can be done at half speed with good results. Also most teams—whether high school, college, or pro—have two sets of defensive backs, totaling six players. So this drill gives everybody on the defensive team a chance to practice.

SIDELINE TACKLING DRILL

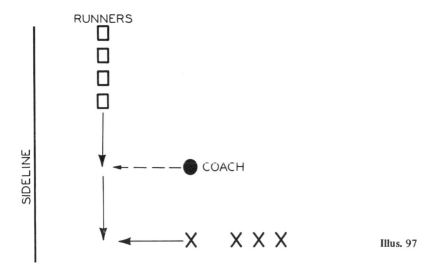

Illus. 97

The purpose of this drill is to teach defensive players sideline and open-field tackling.

INSTRUCTIONS

1. Assign at least three or four offensive backs as runners. Use reserve offensive personnel for this.

2. Let the defensive backfield coach throw the ball to the runner, who tries to go down the sideline.

3. Position all the defensive backs in one line on defense. Make sure that each back gets at least three good shots at a ball carrier.

4. Have the defensive back make the tackle or knock the ball carrier out of bounds.

5. Tell him to push the ball carrier out of bounds as a last resort, and only if it is impossible for him to get his head in front of the runner.

6. See Illustration 97.

CROSSROAD DRILL

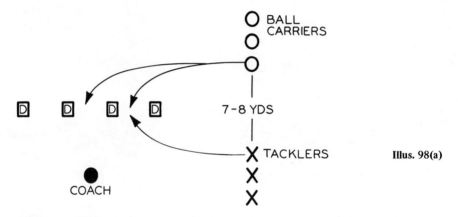

Illus. 98(a)

The purpose of this drill is to enable defensive players to practice open-field tackling, and to emphasize the importance of good body position when a tackler is hitting.

INSTRUCTIONS

1. Line up ball carriers behind three or four bell-bottom dummies, placed 5 yards apart.

2. Have the defensive backs line up about 7 or 8 yards from the dummies.

3. Let the ball carriers run between any of the dummies. If you wish, you may indicate the area you want the ball carrier to go through.

4. Have both the tackler and the runner approach the designated area at the same time, with the tackler keeping an inside position so that the runner cannot cut back. The tackler must be on balance and under control as he tries to meet the runner at the "crossroad."

152   Tackling drills

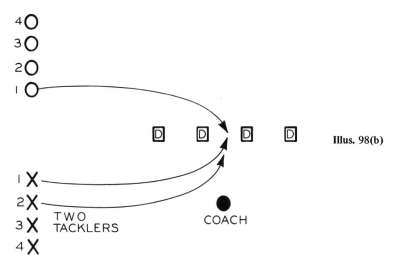

Illus. 98(b)

5. Have the tackler drive his right shoulder and head in front of the runner. He should lock his arms and lift upward at the same time, so that he drives the runner to the ground.

6. After the defensive backs have had two right-shoulder tackles, switch the ball carriers to the left side of the dummies so that the defenders get practice in left-shoulder tackles.

7. You can vary this drill by having two men tackle the ball carrier, with the second player attempting to jar the ball loose from the runner's grasp. Let the first player in line always be the one who tries to make the tackle.

8. See the two parts of Illustration 98.

154   Tackling drills

ON-BALANCE DRILL

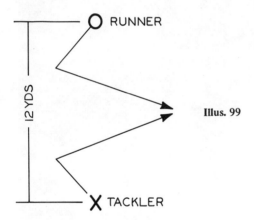

RUNNER

12 YDS

Illus. 99

X TACKLER

The purpose of this drill is to give the deep backs practice in open-field tackling.

INSTRUCTIONS

1. Station reserve runners on offense and deep backs on defense, at least 12 yards apart.

2. Have the deep back sprint forward toward the runner 8 yards before he slows down to get "on balance" and position himself to make the tackle.

3. Allow the ball carrier to make only two fakes, at most.

4. See Illustration 99.

Comment: This drill will prove to the defensive backs that if they are not "on balance" and under control, they are most likely to miss the tackle.

MULTIPLE-BLOCKER DRILL

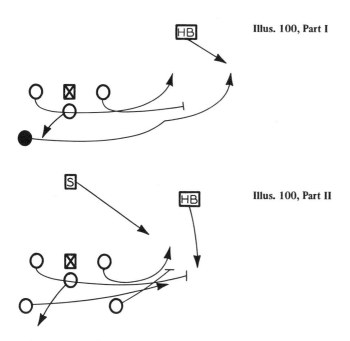

Illus. 100, Part I

Illus. 100, Part II

The purpose of this drill is to teach the defensive players open-field tackling while meeting more than one blocker.

INSTRUCTIONS

1. Arrange to have two blockers (guards) on offense, with a center, ball carrier, and quarterback.

2. Station a deep back on defense in his regular position.

3. Have both guards pull out and lead the play. The ball carrier may cut inside or outside.

4. This drill provides the defender with quite an obstacle: playing two blockers and making the tackle.

5. The second phase of this drill is to add another offensive back, so that three blockers now lead the play.

6. Station another tackler on defense, so that now the drill consists of 3 on 2. Work on change of pace, position on runner, and angle of pursuit.

7. See the two parts of Illustration 100.

LEATHER DRILL

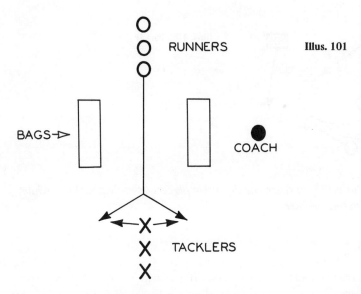

RUNNERS   Illus. 101

BAGS

COACH

TACKLERS

The purpose of this drill is to teach the defensive backs to come forward and make a tackle near the line of scrimmage or at the hole.

INSTRUCTIONS

1. Place two blocking dummies lengthwise on the ground, 4 yards apart.

2. Line up the defensive backs about 6 yards deep.

3. Station the ball carriers 3 yards from the ends of the dummies.

4. Have each defender come up fast, but under control, meet the oncoming runner, and "put the leather to him."

5. See Illustration 101.

CHEEK-TO-CHEEK DRILL

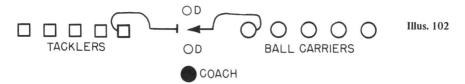

Illus. 102

The object of this drill is to improve the tackling ability of the deep backs and line-backers.

INSTRUCTIONS

1. Have the tackler lie on his back, 5 yards from the ball carrier.

2. Have the ball carrier in a reverse position with his back to his adversary. Let him be in a semi-erect position, with a football at his heels.

3. Station two dummies on either side of the ball carrier, 5 yards apart.

4. When you give a signal, let the ball carrier pick up the ball, pivot, and try to avoid the tackler.

5. Have the tackler spring quickly to his feet and meet the runner.

6. See Illustration 102.

Comment: This is an excellent drill to teach agility, balance, and tackling.

CHAPTER 9

POSITION-ON-RECEIVER DRILLS

Practically every drill offers the deep backs opportunities to improve in more than one way. To improve an individual player's shortcomings, the coach should emphasize one specific skill at a time. This method of teaching is slow, but is fundamentally sound and is the only way to instruct inexperienced pass defenders.

Because today's pass receivers are taller and bigger than ever before, the pass defender's position in relation to the receiver is more important than ever. Proper position on the receiver allows the pass defender to do three things:

1. Intercept the pass.
2. Break up the pass.
3. Tackle the receiver.

When the pass defense coach uses these drills, he should have just one objective in mind: to emphasize position on the receiver. If the coach does not keep this objective constantly in the foreground, the drills will lose their value. Many reaction drills, playing-the-ball drills, and position-on-the-receiver drills are interchangeable.

POSITION DRILL

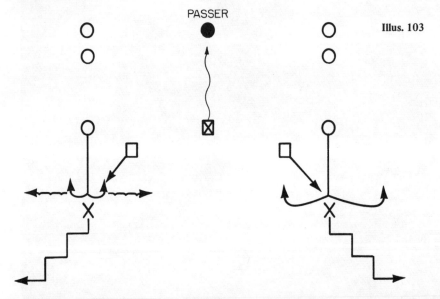

The purpose of this drill is to teach defensive players proper position on the receiver.

INSTRUCTIONS

1. Station one player on offense and one on defense.

2. Limit the offensive player to outside moves first. Then combine these moves with out-and-up moves. Let the offensive man cut shallow, medium, or deep.

3. Later in the drill, have the offensive man add the hook, and then the hook-and-go plus the curl (see Glossary). Also, as a change, to keep the defender honest, have the offensive man run an "up" pattern, commencing with a stutter step (or fake step).

4. To keep the emphasis where you want it, on coverage and position on the receiver, begin by *not* using a football.

5. After the defenders have started maintaining good position on the receiver, add a passer and a football. A center is optional.

6. Emphasize to each defender that he must try to stick to an outside position on the offensive man and not allow the receiver to get closer to him than 3 yards.

7. The preferable defender-to-receiver distance ratio is 1 yard outside and 3 yards deep.

8. See Illustration 103.

Comment: This is a one-on-one position drill, which allows you to combine practice in coverage with practice in the playing of the ball. It is also a simple fundamental drill that should be repeated every practice period.

ONE-ON-ONE DRILL

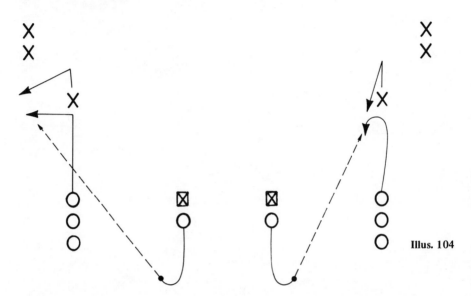

Illus. 104

The purpose of this drill is to give your defenders practice in covering an out.

INSTRUCTIONS

1. Station two lines of receivers on offense.

2. Station two lines of defenders on defense.

3. If possible, have two centers and two quarterbacks to throw passes (although this is not really necessary).

4. Have the receivers run only one pattern: outs. They may run the outs at any depth.

5. Have them run outs first on one side and then on the other side. In this way a coach stationed downfield can check the defenders in both lines for footwork and position.

6. See Illustration 104.

Comment: This is a good drill that can be used all season long to improve the fundamentals of pass defense until the defenders have reached the point where they keep proper position on the receiver.

SPECIAL-PATTERNS DRILL

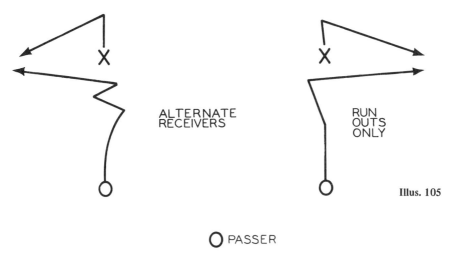

ALTERNATE RECEIVERS

RUN OUTS ONLY

Illus. 105

O PASSER

The purpose of this drill is to enable defensive players to practice defending a special pattern, or maneuver, and to devote enough time to perfecting details of coverage.

INSTRUCTIONS

1. Have two defenders on defense; a good place to station them would be the left and right corners of the field, for example.

2. Station a receiver opposite each defender, but alternate running them. In this way you can check the coverage of first one and then the other.

3. Have the receivers run 15- to 20-yard outs, and no other maneuver. Do not switch to any other pattern until the defenders have perfected their coverage of outs. Add a passer and football later, when you feel that enough progress has been made.

4. See Illustration 105.

Comment: This is a fine drill for spring practice and early fall sessions. However, it serves at any time to sharpen coverage.

Position-on-receiver drills

CENTERFIELDER'S-TURN DRILL

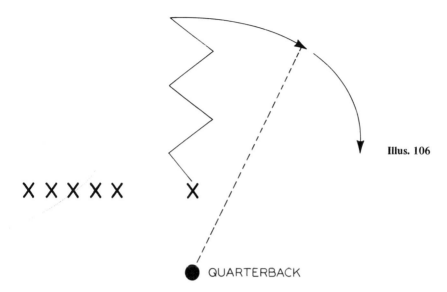

Illus. 106

X X X X X   X   QUARTERBACK

The purpose of this drill is to teach the pass defender to turn the way a centerfielder does when the ball is thrown behind him.

INSTRUCTIONS

1. Line up the pass defenders in single file.

2. Use a reserve quarterback for this drill, because you want long passes.

3. Have the quarterback, by faking passes first in one direction and then the other, make the defender turn four or five times. Finally, when the defender has his back to the passer, have the passer throw the ball back behind the defender.

4. Insist that the defender use the centerfielder's turn and take his eyes off the passer and ball. If he does this correctly, he can gain one or two steps, besides putting himself in a better position to play the ball. This is better than trying to open hips and cross over (see Glossary).

5. As soon as he makes his turn, have him take a *quick* look at the ball. Many times a defender does not look quickly enough and the pass is completed before he has seen it.

6. See Illustration 106.

Comment: This is a good drill. Defenders need work on this type of pass so that they will be in the proper position when they encounter one in a game.

PLAYING-THROUGH-THE-RECEIVER DRILL

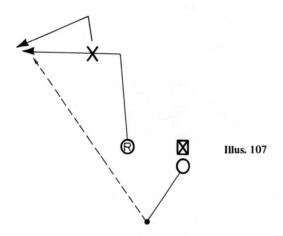

Illus. 107

The purpose of this drill is to teach the defender to play the ball through the receiver and to play it at its highest point.

INSTRUCTIONS

1. Station one halfback on defense at his normal position and depth.

2. Use a center, passer, and receiver on offense.

3. Have the receiver run down and out patterns and have the passer "hang" the ball outside.

4. Tell the defender to *play through* the receiver, or go for the ball as though the receiver weren't even there, and intercept the ball at its highest point.

5. See Illustration 107.

TWO-ON-ONE DRILL

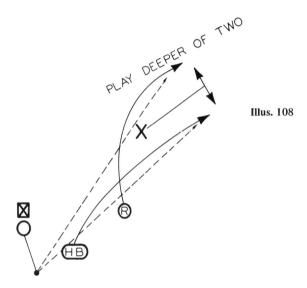

PLAY DEEPER OF TWO

Illus. 108

The purpose of this drill is to teach the pass defender to always play the deeper man in his zone.

INSTRUCTIONS

1. Station a receiver, halfback, center, and quarterback on offense. Let two receivers release on every pass, one going deep and one short.

2. Use a cornerman on defense to cover his one-third zone.

3. Have the end be the offensive man that usually goes deep, so that the defender has to cover him first, and then come forward if the ball is thrown to the halfback (who is playing short).

4. See Illustration 108.

Comment: This drill teaches the defender that the more *width* he keeps, the better position he will be in to cover both receivers.

MAN-FOR-MAN-COVERAGE DRILL

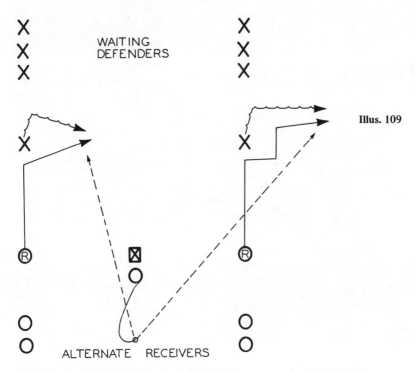

Illus. 109

WAITING
DEFENDERS

ALTERNATE   RECEIVERS

The purpose of this drill is to enable players to practice individual coverage and at the same time tackling of offensive receivers.

INSTRUCTIONS

1. Station two lines of receivers on the offensive, with a center and quarterback.

2. Use two lines of defensive backs, who are to cover the receivers without any help.

3. Have the receivers run any maneuver they choose; the quarterback always throws the ball.

4. Unless two coaches are present, one to watch each line, alternate sides.

5. See Illustration 109.

Comment: This drill combines running with the ball after intercepting (or receiving) and tackling a ball carrier.

POSITION AND FLOW DRILL

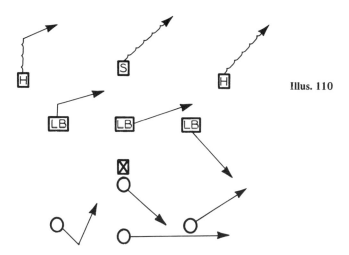

Illus. 110

The purpose of this drill is to teach defensive players how to maintain correct position on the receivers when there is flow action.

INSTRUCTIONS

1. Station three deep backs and three linebackers on defense.

2. Employ a center and two or three backs on offense.

3. Use men in motion and flankers with flow action (see Glossary).

4. Be sure to give the defense time to adjust. Many times the crew running the offensive will try to get in too many plays by hurrying them, and the defense does not have time to adjust. It is better to run fewer plays and make certain everyone is in the proper position.

5. After the defensive players have begun to play in their correct positions, let the plays be run faster.

6. See Illustration 110.

PLAYING-A-BALL-FROM-THE-OUTSIDE DRILL

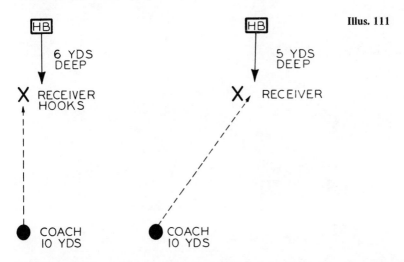

Illus. 111

The purpose of this drill is to give the defender practice in playing a sideline pass from the outside.

INSTRUCTIONS

1. Station a receiver downfield in a position to receive an out.

2. Locate a defender approximately 5 yards behind the receiver and 1 yard to the outside.

3. Position yourself (or a passer) 10 yards from the *of* defensive player. Throw the ball slightly to the outside of the receiver.

4. Let the defender try to intercept or break up the pass.

5. Occasionally throw the ball directly at the defender, to make sure he is not focusing too much attention on the receiver.

6. You can vary this drill by stationing a hook man downfield and throwing the ball directly into the numbers. Let the defender again be slightly to the outside of the receiver.

7. See Illustration 111.

Comment: This drill is a difficult one for the defenders.

POST-PRACTICE DRILL

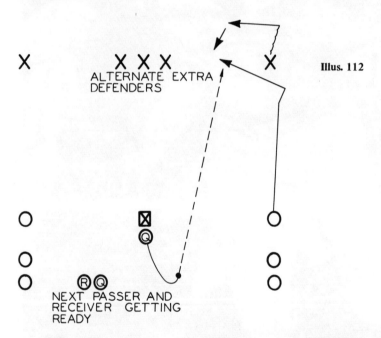

Illus. 112

ALTERNATE EXTRA
DEFENDERS

NEXT PASSER AND
RECEIVER GETTING
READY

The purpose of this drill is to provide something extra in the way of drill for the receivers and defenders.

INSTRUCTIONS

1. Tell one center, two quarterbacks, a few receivers, and specific pass defenders to remain on the field for 10 minutes after practice is over.

2. Ask certain defensive players who need extra work to remain for this 10-minute period; you can vary the centers and quarterbacks.

3. Explain to the players that this is strictly a one-on-one situation and that it is pure training in coverage for the defense. Tell the defense not to tackle, but just to try to break up every pass.

4. Have the receiver and passer get together before each play and let the receiver call the maneuver he wants to run.

5. Use two quarterbacks; this means that there is no delay, since one group is always ready with a play.

6. Stand at a spot where you can see the defense clearly, and comment on each man's coverage.

7. See Illustration 112.

Comment: Many times more learning and improvement can result from this 10-minute period than from the entire practice session.

BASIC-POSITION DRILL

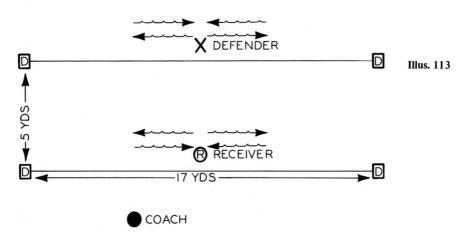

Illus. 113

The purpose of this drill is to teach the defender to keep a fundamental position on the receiver, and also to improve his footwork and lateral agility.

INSTRUCTIONS

1. Place one pass defender on a line and station a receiver opposite him. The distance between the two players should not be less than 5 yards.

2. Station four dummies at the end of the lines 17 yards apart.

3. Tell the offensive player he has to stay on his line. He should move laterally back and forth as quickly as possible.

4. Tell the defensive player to try to remain in front of the offensive player, matching each movement.

5. After several sideways moves back and forth, give a verbal command and let the receiver cross the defender's line. The defender must cover him as he breaks downfield.

6. See Illustration 113.

CHAPTER 10

PLAY-RECOGNITION DRILLS

Because of their importance, play recognition drills should take up part of the pass defense practice time. Every defensive back requires training of this kind. In addition, you will find that training your men in play recognition is most gratifying, because you can readily note improvement in most individuals. Occasionally you find an over-aggressive defender who can be fooled repeatedly, however, no matter how much training you give him.

Good play recognition drills are scarce, and to drill just for the sake of drilling is useless. A coach should put much thought into any drill before he uses it, and this is especially true with play recognition drills.

During the season it is almost impossible for a coach to find enough time on the defensive practice schedule for all types of drills. The best time to teach play recognition is during spring practice, and when working on double sessions early in the fall before classes start. Of course, the true test and the best drills come through scrimmaging under game conditions. But this kind of practice should come after a coach has first given individual and sectional drills.

There are 16 play recognition drills in this chapter. We have used all of them at one time or another while coaching in college and in the National Football League.

PASS-RUN REACTION DRILL

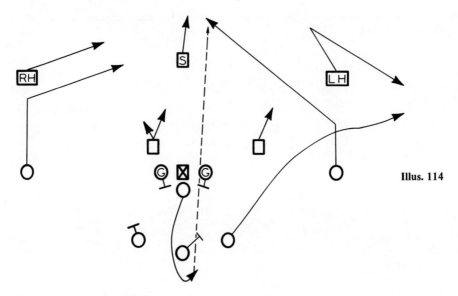

Illus. 114

The purpose of this drill is to enable defensive players to practice keying for a pass or run and to provide the secondary with practice in tackling.

INSTRUCTIONS

1. Place a complete secondary of three or four halfbacks on defense. Use at least two linebackers.

2. Use a center, quarterback, three backs, two ends, and two guards on offense.

3. Tell the players to put the emphasis on passing, with just enough running to keep the defenders honest.

4. If the guards block aggressively or *pull,* let them come up to make the tackle. If they pass-block, let the defenders cover the ends.

5. See Illustration 114.

Comment: This drill teaches the secondary to figure out whether a given play is going to be a pass or a run.

READING DRILL

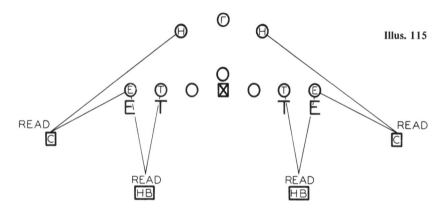

The purpose of this drill is to teach the players to "read" or "key" their opponents first, and then look for the football.

INSTRUCTIONS

1. Arrange an entire offensive team opposite four deep backs.

2. Use tall standing dummies to occupy the positions of defensive ends and tackles.

3. Have the offensive team use passing plays, with an occasional run to keep the defense honest.

4. Make sure that the players read their men first before they search for the ball.

5. See Illustration 115.

READING-THE-CENTER DRILL

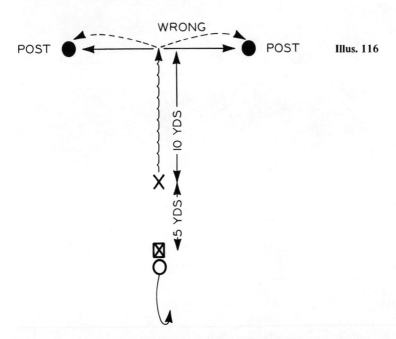

WRONG

POST

POST

Illus. 116

10 YDS

5 YDS

The purpose of this drill is to enable the defensive players to practice playing the field and reading the block of the center.

INSTRUCTIONS

1. Station a center and quarterback on offense.

2. Locate two dummies 15 yards downfield, as stationary receivers.

3. Station a defensive back in the middle, 5 yards deep. Have the back read the block of the center and then sprint back, using whatever footwork you think is correct. When he reaches a point 10 yards deep, he should be facing the passer.

4. Let the passer throw to either post man and the defender try to break up the pass. Gradually widen the posts as the players increase their lateral interception distance.

5. Be prepared for the fact that the defender will usually *not* be under control at 10 yards, as he will probably break at the wrong angle, or take an extra step. That is, momentum may carry him back too far, or his footwork in stopping and moving laterally to cover the receiver may not be correct. (The correct angle is shown by the solid line at the top of Illustration 116.)

6. See Illustration 116.

Comment: This drill is also a good one for linebackers.

KEYING DRILL

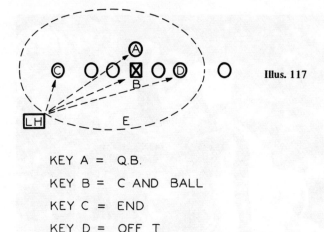

Illus. 117

KEY A = Q.B.

KEY B = C AND BALL

KEY C = END

KEY D = OFF T

KEY E = ALL A,B,C,D

The purpose of this drill is to give the defensive backs practice in keying specific offensive players and to help them develop peripheral vision.

INSTRUCTIONS

1. Station seven linemen and a quarterback on offense, and let them run through several plays.

2. Have one or two backs at a time station themselves in their usual defensive positions, and—by watching the various "keys" to what the offensive players are going to do—try to determine whether the upcoming play will be a pass or a run.

3. Explain that the four keys are: the offensive quarterback's eyes, the way the center handles the football, the offensive receiver, and the offside tackle.

4. Insist that each player watch his keys in the proper order; otherwise he will be in trouble.

5. Have some of the players active in teaching these keys, while the others remain inactive and watch.

6. See Illustration 117.

Comment: Good defenders, with practice and experience, can learn to watch all four things at once, using peripheral vision.

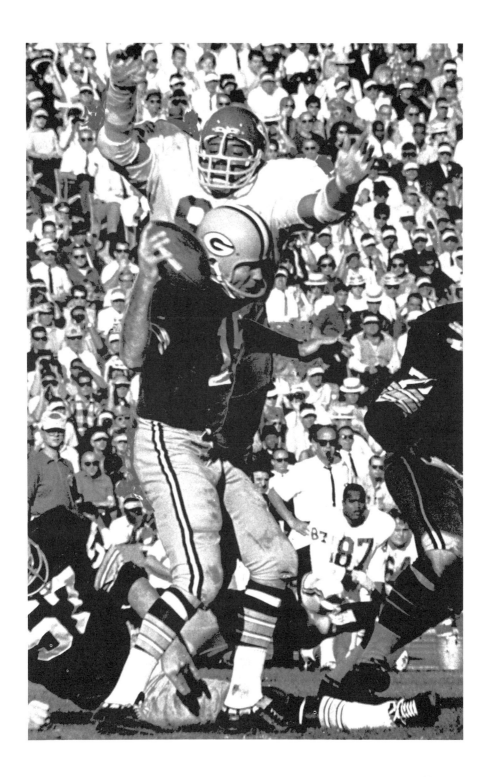

CROSS-FIELD-COVERAGE DRILL

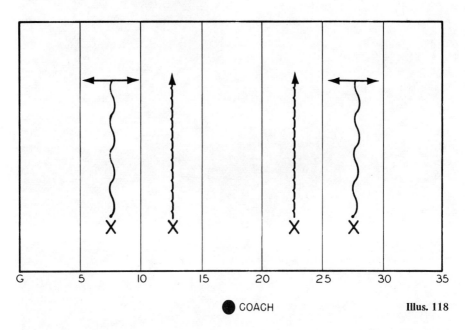

Illus. 118

The purpose of this drill, which is really three drills in one, is to train the deep backs in getting back and covering their zones.

INSTRUCTIONS

1. Start this drill in a 20-yard area, and gradually increase to a 50-yard area. By using the field from sideline to sideline, you can give your players a feeling for the width, in yards, that they are responsible for.

2. Station players in their defensive positions facing you, or a quarterback, on the sideline. To start with, use at least four defenders. You may add linebackers later.

3. Use hand signals to make the players turn from one side to another, until they reach their zones. Keep in mind the coaching points in this drill: a player's stance, his footwork on the way to his zone, his changing of direction *after* he reaches his zone, and his continual watching of the passer.

4. After the players reach the desired depth, again use hand motions to move them laterally in their zones.

5. After they have covered the full width of the field, bring them back from the opposite side in the same manner.

6. Use the same drill again, but this time take an offensive end and have the defender stay with him. Let the receiver change direction all the way across the field, but remain in the defender's zone.

7. Repeat the same drill, but this time station two defenders on defense so that they can practice working together. Place the left corner and left safety man together, for example, to develop teamwork.

8. Add a passer to the drill and have him throw to the receiver. Again let the receiver remain within the two zones; let the passer throw long, short, and medium-length passes. Tell the passer to wait, most of the time, until the defender reaches the center of his zone.

9. See Illustration 118.

Comment: The last part of this drill gives the defender practice in playing the ball, intercepting, and blocking back on the receiver.

COVERING-THE-FIELD DRILL

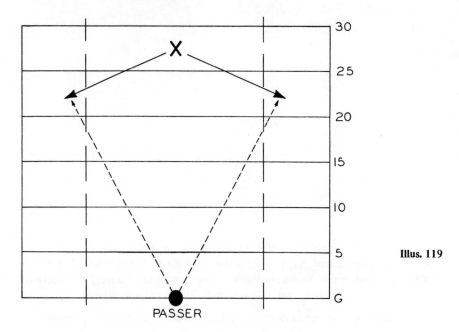

Illus. 119

The purpose of this drill is to provide practice for the defensive backs in covering the football field.

INSTRUCTIONS

1. Station one defender 25 yards deep downfield. Have him stand between the hash marks and assume his defensive stance.

2. Get a reserve quarterback to stand on the goal line and throw passes aimed at spots from one side of the field to the other. To extend the defender's coverage, let each pass be wider than the one before.

3. By gradually increasing the defender's reach, the quarterback will also increase the defender's confidence in his ability to cover.

4. When the passer throws the ball outside the hash marks, have him "lay the ball up" (i.e., let him lob it or lay it up softly—not fire it) so that the defender has a chance to intercept.

5. See Illustration 119.

SAFETY-KEYING DRILL

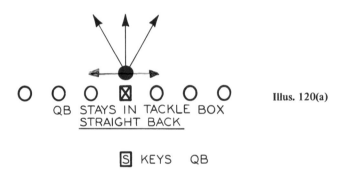

Illus. 120(a)

QB STAYS IN TACKLE BOX
STRAIGHT BACK

⬛ KEYS   QB

The purpose of this drill is to provide practice for the safety men in recognizing plays in advance, and in classifying the actions of the quarterback.

INSTRUCTIONS

1. Station the safety man on defense by himself.

2. Tell the safety man that, in all the backfield action that he is about to see, he must *key the quarterback.*

3. Part 1 of this drill consists of stationing a quarterback on offense, with 7 offensive linemen. Let the linemen simulate pass-blocking and the ends hold their ground.

4. Have the quarterback use drop-back action on all his passes and not go outside the tackle box (or blocking cup).

SAFETY-KEYING DRILL (continued)

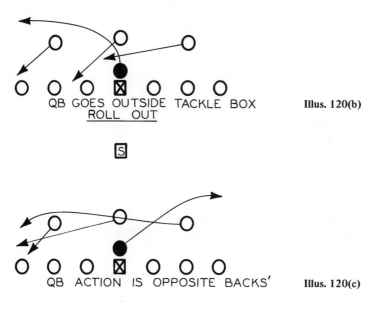

QB GOES OUTSIDE TACKLE BOX
ROLL OUT

Illus. 120(b)

QB ACTION IS OPPOSITE BACKS'

Illus. 120(c)

5.　In part 2 of the drill, station three offensive backs with the quarterback, and let the quarterback use roll-out passes, past the tackle box.

6.　In part 3 of this drill, have the quarterback go in the opposite direction from the rest of the backs.

7.　Size up the situation; you should be able to tell whether the "play action" of the other backs is bothering the quarterback; the safeties must not be fooled by this "play action," either.

8.　See the three parts of Illustration 120.

Comment:　This drill, which consists of three separate parts, is a good early-season drill.

KEYING-THE-END DRILL

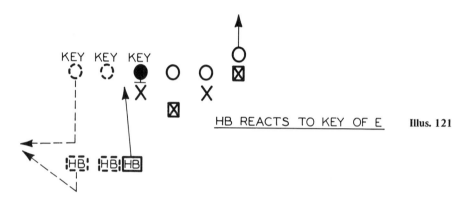

HB REACTS TO KEY OF E   **Illus. 121**

The purpose of this drill is to provide training for the halfback in keying or reading the end.

INSTRUCTIONS

1. Station a single halfback on defense, with two linemen and a linebacker.

2. Station a skeleton crew consisting of a center, guard, tackle, a quarterback, and an end on offense.

3. Move the end to varying distances from the rest of the linemen, so that he is at one time wide, another time medium, another time tight.

4. Tell the halfback always to key the widest man on his side of the field.

5. Have the end fake a block and the off-tackle (i.e., the tackle who is stationed on the side away from the play) come downfield. Let the halfback then come forward to meet the run.

6. Next, have the end release downfield. Then let the defensive halfback, instead of continuing to cover the end, transfer his key to the quarterback.

7. See Illustration 121.

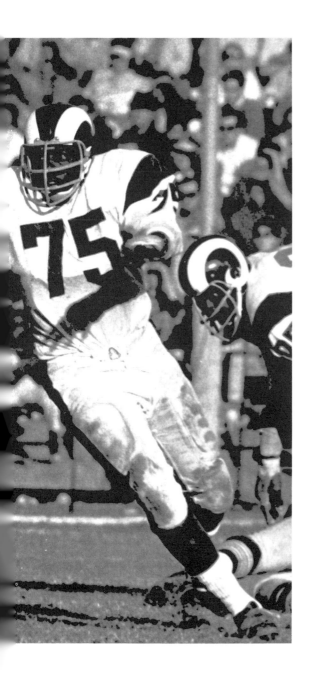

THREE-KEY READING DRILL

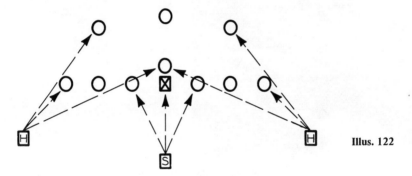

Illus. 122

The purpose of this drill is to provide practice for the secondary in reading their opponents' actions as cues to the next play.

INSTRUCTIONS

1. Station eleven players on offense (use a reserve unit).

2. Station 3 or 4 deep backs on defense.

3. Get the offensive team to run through a number of plays (pass plays and running plays).

4. Have the halfbacks practice reading the quarterback, end, and halfback, in that order.

5. Have the safety practice reading the quarterback, center, and guards, in that order.

6. See Illustration 122.

SAFETY-HALFBACK COVERAGE DRILL

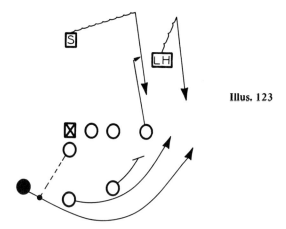

Illus. 123

The purpose of this drill is to teach coordination between the safety man and the halfback on runs and passes.

INSTRUCTIONS

1. Line up an offensive unit consisting of a center, guard, tackle, and a complete backfield on offense.

2. Station a halfback and a safety man on defense.

3. Have the end come downfield. Tell the halfback to be sure the safety man moves laterally before he comes up to tackle the runner.

4. Have both defenders play everything as a pass *first* and a run second. When the halfback is supporting on a run, have him come up from the outside toward the inside. Let the safety man move over and be in position to make the tackle when the runner is forced inside by the halfback.

5. See Illustration 123.

PROJECTOR DRILL

The purpose of this drill is to train men to recognize plays in advance when they are viewing film.

INSTRUCTIONS

1. Use this drill in team meetings when the defensive backs are studying film.

2. Have the defenders call out "pass" or "run" before a play has completely developed.

3. Do not run the play through, but keep reversing the film just after it shows the snap of the ball.

4. This is a good drill to keep the defensive backs alert in team meetings, as well as to teach them play recognition.

STAY-AT-HOME DRILL

The purpose of this drill is to train the deep backs and linebackers to stay at home and protect their territory. This is an excellent drill to keep players from being lured into chasing backs who are faking.

INSTRUCTIONS

1. Station a complete team of eleven players on offense.

2. Station a complete team of eleven players on defense.

3. Have the offensive team run through their regular plays. Have the defensive team watch them, and react to these plays.

4. After several plays, have the offense run through a pass play *without the football.*

5. Watch the deep backs' reactions. If a deep back comes up to stop a run and finds that he has lost the ball, he will remember this in the future.

Comment: This drill is an excellent one for the deep backs, and always provides several laughs.

COVERING-WIDTH-OF-FIELD DRILL

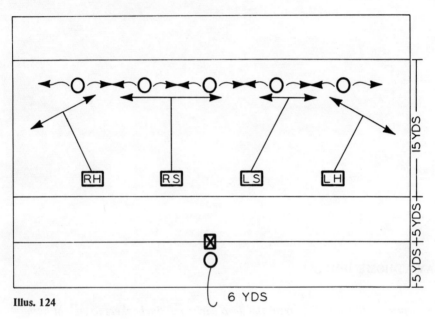

Illus. 124

6 YDS

The purpose of this drill is to teach the defenders that they can cover the entire width of the football field.

INSTRUCTIONS

1. Station five receivers downfield at a distance of 20 yards from the quarterback.

2. Station your deep backs on defense in their normal positions, approximately five yards from the passer.

3. Locate a quarterback on offense, with or without a center. Have him retreat and throw to one of the five receivers.

4. Have the defenders go backward as the quarterback sets up to pass.

5. Note that if the pass defenders do a good job, they will be able to break up most of the passes thrown.

6. See Illustration 124.

PATTERN-RECOGNITION DRILL

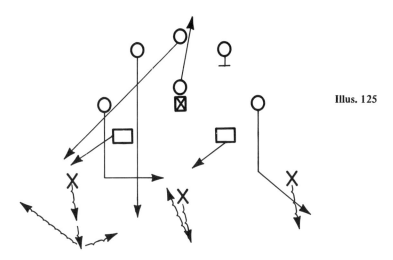

Illus. 125

The purpose of this drill is to teach players to recognize the pass patterns.

INSTRUCTIONS

1. Station on offense a skeleton crew consisting of a center, a quarterback, two ends, and three backs.

2. Station on defense three pass defenders and two or three linebackers.

3. Have the offense run the opponents' key pass patterns. Have the defense try to recognize the patterns and call them out.

4. See Illustration 125.

Comment: This drill, in addition to emphasizing pass pattern recognition, also gives players practice in maintaining proper position on the receiver.

198 Play-recognition drills

CHAPTER 11

SECTIONAL DRILLS

The 23 sectional drills that follow could be included in the chapter on team drills. However, because of the tremendous importance of sectional drills, a separate chapter is devoted entirely to their application.

We believe that the best and fastest way to teach pass defense is by the use of sectional drills. These drills offer the linebackers and deep backs an opportunity to improve in several ways. In addition, they serve to develop *teamwork,* which is vital to pass defense.

Sectional drills should come after a coach has first trained the players individually. The individual's shortcomings are revealed in these sectional drills. Then the coach may give additional training to the various players by means of solo drilling.

After the football season starts, the coach should place more emphasis on sectional drills and less on individual drills. He should stress individual drilling in the spring and in the early fall practice.

Not all these drills will fit into everyone's program. The coach should evaluate them, and select those which seem to best answer the needs of his defensive personnel.

LINEBACKER TEAMWORK DRILL

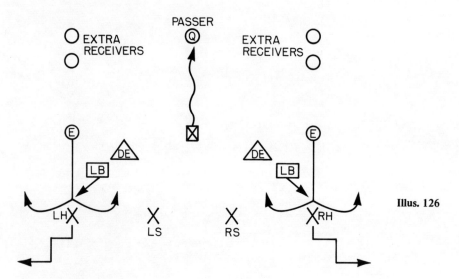

Illus. 126

The purpose of this drill is to develop coordination between the deep backs, line-backers, and ends.

INSTRUCTIONS

1. Station four deep backs on defense against an offensive backfield with ends.

2. Station two defensive ends with one, two, or three linebackers.

3. Have one coach working with the four deep backs. Have another coach working with the defensive ends and the linebackers.

4. Let the ends concentrate on maintaining an outside position when they are rushing the passer. Let them also work with the linebackers on stunts.

5. Encourage the deep backs to develop teamwork with both defensive ends and linebackers.

6. See Illustration 126.

Comment: This drill is one that is often overlooked.

DEEP-BACK AND LINEBACKER DRILL

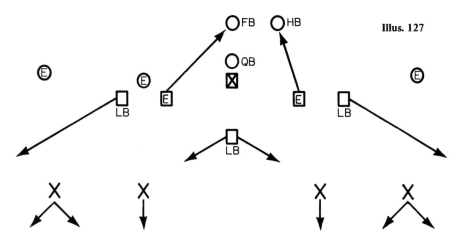

Illus. 127

The purpose of this drill is to enable pass defenders to practice working with line-backers.

INSTRUCTIONS

1. Station one, two, three, or four defenders on pass defense.

2. Station one, two, or three linebackers on defense with the pass defenders.

3. Line up an offensive team consisting of at least a center and quarterback and two pass receivers.

4. Limit the moves of the offensive receivers to inside hooks and outs, along with curls, since the idea behind this drill is to perfect the defenders' coverage of these specific moves.

5. Have the defenders communicate with the linebackers one at a time; this is an essential in good pass coverage.

6. See Illustration 127.

Comment: This is an excellent drill for linebackers as well as deep backs, and one that is often overlooked or practiced in the wrong relationship. By practicing with just this segment of your defensive team, you will get proper concentration.

PROPER-DISTANCE DRILL

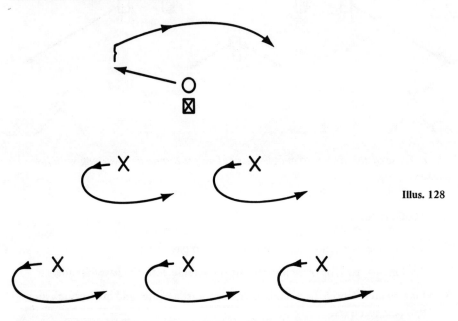

Illus. 128

The purpose of this drill is to make the deep backs conscious of maintaining proper distance between themselves and the next man, and between themselves and the sideline, when they are rotating.

INSTRUCTIONS

1. Station three deep backs and two linebackers on defense, with a center and quarterback on offense.

2. First direct the defenders, by hand motions with a football, to rotate as shown in Illustration 128.

3. When you slap the football, have everyone stop where he is and check the distance between himself and the next player, and also between himself and the sideline.

4. Have the quarterback drop back and roll out left and right, faking but not actually passing.

5. Let him start one way and come back in the opposite direction, so that your secondary has to perform the most difficult type of pass coverage: covering a quarterback who "scrambles" all over the field.

6. After the defenders get the proper perspective on this drill, have the passer throw the ball. This gives the defenders practice in converging on the ball and forming a wall.

7. See Illustration 128.

SEVEN-ON-SEVEN DRILL

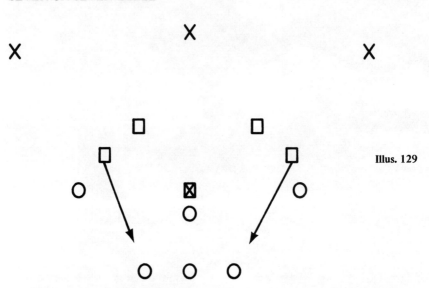

Illus. 129

The purpose of this drill is to give the defensive players and also the offensive ones valuable training without scrimmaging.

INSTRUCTIONS

1. Station seven players on offense: a center, a quarterback, two ends, and three backs. This is a live drill except that the secondary does not do any tackling.

2. Line up the following players on defense: two defensive ends, two linebackers, and three defenders.

3. Have the offense throw passes, with an occasional end run to keep the defensive ends honest. Tell the offense to use screens and draws (see Glossary).

4. Remove all other players from the playing field and have a manager keep time. Use a regular system of downs and yardage requirements, so that both offensive and defensive quarterbacks can make calls under gamelike conditions.

5. Have the offensive team use its own pass patterns and the defensive team use its own defensive tactics.

6. Let the defensive secondary get practice in covering, playing the ball, and returning intercepted passes, and the defensive end get practice in rushing the passer.

7. Let the offensive backs get practice in blocking for the passer, and the passer get training in timing, in hitting his receivers, and in staying in the cup.

8. You can vary this drill by having the offense use opponents' patterns and having the defense practice its own defensive tactics against these plays. Or you can have the offense use its own patterns and the defense use opponents' defensive tactics.

9. See Illustration 129.

Comment: This drill gives you seven players on offense and seven on defense, and one of the finest skeleton drills in football.

CROSSING-PATTERNS DRILL

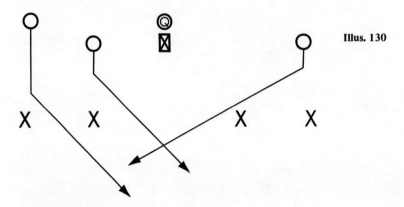

Illus. 130

The purpose of this drill is to enable defensive players to practice against a strong-side line pattern.

INSTRUCTIONS

1. Station three receivers, a center, and a quarterback on offense. Alternate the strong side on every play, but see to it that there are some end runs on the weak side.

2. Position four defensive backs on defense; do not use linebackers.

3. Have the offense use only those crossing patterns that you expect your opponents to use. Have the defenders make their calls and play the pass defense patterns full tilt.

4. See Illustration 130.

Comment: Depending on the type of coverage you employ, this drill is a good one to eliminate confusion and give the secondary confidence in their ability to cover passes and in their ability to work together. If you are using zone coverage as a defensive tactic, this drill enables you to see whether the defenders are staying with their men too long.

POSITION-ON-WHISTLE DRILL

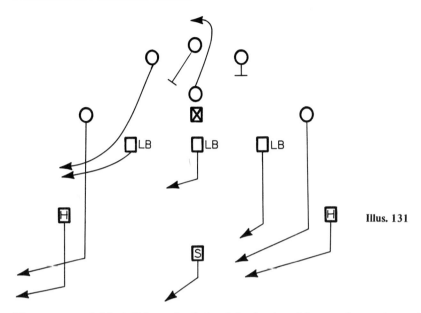

The purpose of this drill is to check the defenders' position on the receivers when the coach blows his whistle.

INSTRUCTIONS

1. Station a center, a complete backfield, and two ends on offense.

2. Locate three pass defenders and three linebackers on defense, or any other variation you wish.

3. Have the offense throw all types of passes, with emphasis on those pass patterns that you expect opponents to use.

4. Let the defense concentrate on recognizing each pass pattern and getting the right position of each defender on that pattern.

5. Use defensive ends in this drill, to give them practice in rushing and blocking. This drill also gives the offensive line practice in blocking.

6. Depending on the pattern, blow your whistle at 5, 10, or 15 yards. At this signal, have everyone on offense and defense stop immediately. You then check the defensive players' positions on the receivers.

7. See Illustration 131.

Comment: This is a drill to use after you have drilled players in position on the individual receiver, rather than position in a zone.

THREE-AND-FOUR-DEEP ALIGNMENT DRILL

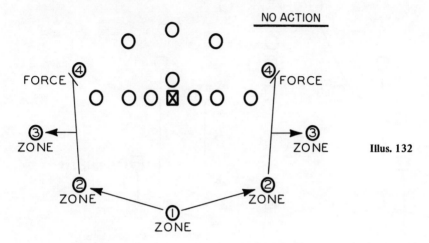

Illus. 132

The purpose of this drill is to enable the pass defenders to visualize, by means of charts, what their movements and their responsibilities should be, and to see how their movements are coordinated in the total defense.

INSTRUCTIONS

1. Use this as a blackboard drill to give each defender a mental picture of his responsibilities before he goes out onto the field.

2. Use the drill again when the defenders are on the practice field. Let them run through the drill without any movement on the part of the offensive players, until you feel that they understand what their movements should be.

3. Start with the "three-deep" alignment first, to show the movement of the secondary. Then proceed to the umbrella defense. Since the umbrella defense becomes the three-deep defense on revolves, this drill helps to avoid confusion.

4. Use a numbering system to illustrate the zones as follows: Zone 1 is 12 yards deep from the center and midway between the other two defensive zones. Zone 2 is 8 yards deep and 2 yards outside of the end or the widest player. Zone 3 is 4 yards deep and represents the flat zone. The men who get into Zone 4 are responsible for forcing the offensive backs to make wide runs.

5. See Illustration 132.

BREAKDOWN PASS DEFENSE DRILL

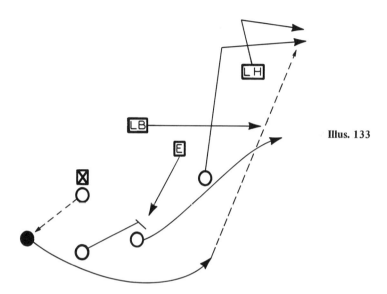

Illus. 133

The purpose of this drill is to enable the defensive players to concentrate on rushing the passer and on practicing specific defense patterns.

INSTRUCTIONS

1. Station a center, quarterback, end, and three backs on offense. Have the offense run wide, pass wide (roll-outs and running passes), and throw hooks. Tell them to attack the right side first.

2. Station on defense a left end, a linebacker, and a left halfback.

3. Let the defensive end practice rushing the passer and forcing plays to go wide. Let the linebacker practice defensing the hooks (that is, setting up defensive measures against "hook" patterns of offensive ends), and the halfback practice covering the receiver on running passes, and also practice coming up to make the tackle from the defensive-back position.

4. Use the same drill on the other side, with the right defensive halfback, linebacker, and right end.

5. You may emphasize any specific pass you wish in this drill.

6. See Illustration 133.

ROLL-OUT DRILL

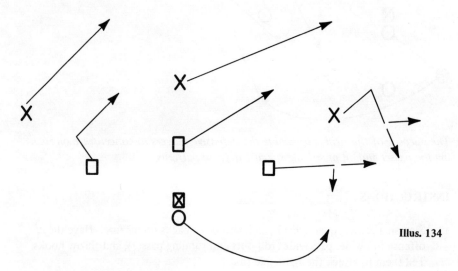

Illus. 134

The purpose of this drill is to enable defensive players to practice working on roll-out pass plays in both directions.

INSTRUCTIONS

1. Station a complete secondary and linebackers on defense. You may add ends later on, to give them practice in containing the passer.

2. Use only a center and quarterback on offense. Do not use receivers.

3. Have the offense make every play a roll-out play.

4. See Illustration 134.

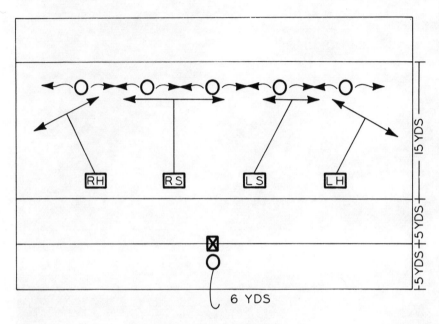

The purpose of this drill is to show the defenders that they can cover the entire width of the playing field.

INSTRUCTIONS

1. Station five receivers 20 yards downfield from the passer. Allow them to move in lateral directions only.

2. Station four deep backs in their normal positions, 5 yards from the passer.

3. As the passer retreats to throw, have the defenders go backward, always keeping their eyes on the passer. Let them play their zones and the field.

4. Have the receivers move left or right, the point being that the defenders do not know exactly where they are located.

5. Let the passer try to complete a pass to one of the receivers, and the defenders try to intercept or break up the pass.

6. Note that this drill requires a good passer; often a coach does the passing in this drill.

7. See Illustration 135.

LOCATING-OPEN-AREA DRILL

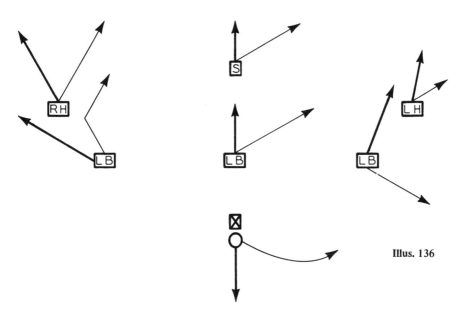

Illus. 136

The purpose of this drill is to give all the secondary men practice in covering the entire field, and in not allowing the ball to hit the ground.

INSTRUCTIONS

1. Station the defensive backs and linebackers on defense. If defensive ends figure in your pass coverage, use them also.

2. Use a center and reserve quarterback. Have the quarterback set up to pass and try to throw to an open area. Let the pass defenders try to keep the ball from striking the ground.

3. Have the defensive men use all their calls, and practice only their own defenses.

4. Tell the quarterback to drop straight back, roll out right, roll out left, and scramble.

5. See Illustration 136.

OVERLAPPING-ZONES DRILL

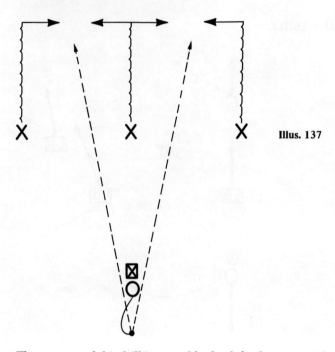

Illus. 137

The purpose of this drill is to enable the defenders to practice being in position to overlap each other at all times.

INSTRUCTIONS

1. Station three pass defenders (deep backs) on defense.

2. Use a center and a quarterback on offense. As the passer retreats, have the defenders go back to their zones, each man being responsible for his one-third area.

3. Have the passer throw all his passes between the three defenders. If the right half calls for the ball, let the safety cover him up, or if the safety calls for the ball, let the right half cover up for him.

4. Have the passer occasionally throw outside, near the sideline, to keep the defenders honest, and to see if they are covering their entire zones.

5. See Illustration 137.

THROWBACK DRILL

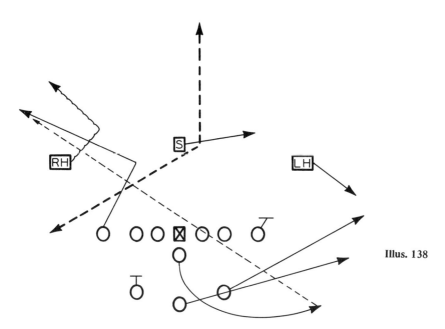

Illus. 138

The purpose of this drill is to enable the off-side cornerman to practice covering the throwback pass.

INSTRUCTIONS

1. Use a complete team on offense. Have them throw transcontinental passes on two out of every four plays.

2. Station three defensive backs in their usual positions.

3. Have the off-side halfback be alert for the throwback, and cover two-thirds of the playing field. (The heavy dashed line in Illustration 138 indicates the area he must cover.)

4. Have the players practice this drill for both left and right sides of the field.

5. See Illustration 138.

SECTIONAL UMBRELLA DRILL

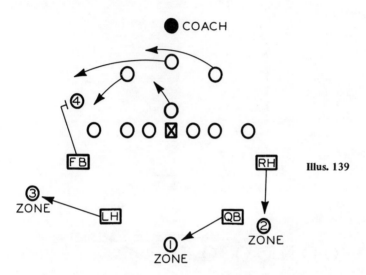

Illus. 139

The purpose of this drill is to enable defensive players to practice revolving from an umbrella defense, at full speed, while playing against an offensive unit.

INSTRUCTIONS

1. Line up a complete secondary on defense, versus a complete offensive unit of eleven players. Use Junior Varsity personnel on offense.

2. Station yourself with the offensive team so that you can direct the plays. Let the offense either run or pass, but get them to emphasize their passing game.

3. Since the offensive linemen do not have anyone to block, let them go through their assignments in such a way that the defensive players can benefit by being able to "read" or "key" the offense.

4. Have the defenders go full speed and try to break up the pass or intercept. Let tackling be optional for the defensive secondary.

5. See Illustration 139.

Comment: This is known as a sectional umbrella drill.

SKELETAL-CUT DRILL

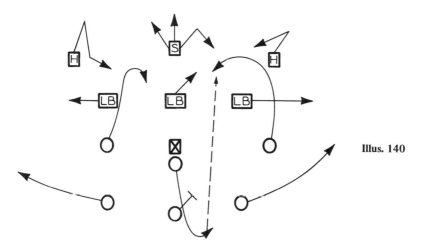

Illus. 140

The purpose of this drill is to enable players to practice all the fundamentals of offense and defense, with competition to motivate them.

INSTRUCTIONS

1. Station two ends, three backs, a quarterback, and a center on offense.

2. Station three linebackers and three deep backs on defense.

3. Let the offense use any cuts or patterns they wish.

4. Let the defense use any defense they wish.

5. Play from the 50-yard line on in.

6. Allow four downs to make first and 10, and let a touchdown count 6 points.

7. Let the defenders get 6 points and have the ball returned to the 50-yard line every time they make an interception. If they bat down a ball, let it count 3 points.

8. Stress all the principles and techniques of pass defense.

9. If you are not using unlimited substitution, let the team making the interception get 3 points and possession of the ball plus gain on return.

10. See Illustration 140.

SPEED DRILL

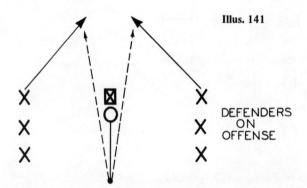

Illus. 141

DEFENDERS
ON
OFFENSE

The purpose of this drill is to provide a warm-up for the defensive backs, while at the same time allowing them to handle the ball as much as possible in a short interval.

INSTRUCTIONS

1. Have all the defenders form two lines on each side of the passer. Use a reserve quarterback if possible in this drill, with a center.

2. As quickly as the quarterback can throw, have the defenders release for a pass.

3. Have the quarterback throw only short passes, and let each defender place the ball next to the center on the ground as he returns.

4. Use plenty of footballs.

5. See Illustration 141.

Comment: This is a fine pregame drill when a team is playing in cold weather, because all the defensive backs are kept active. It is a rapid-fire drill, and it is amazing how many passes each defender can catch and how much running takes place within 2 or 3 minutes. This is also an excellent drill for offensive ends.

PITCH-AND-CATCH DRILL

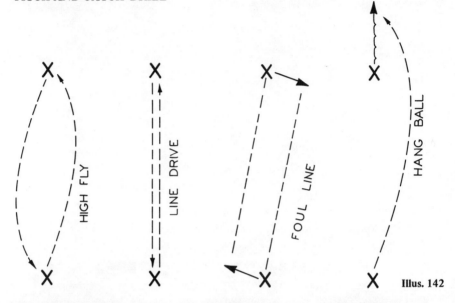

Illus. 142

The purpose of this drill is to provide extra practice in playing the ball for the deep backs and linebackers.

INSTRUCTIONS

1. Move the defensive backs to an open end of the field, so that they have plenty of space.

2. Provide one football for each pair of defensive backs. This allows for rapid-fire interceptions in a short space of time.

3. Have the players throw both long and short interceptions. In addition, have each defender play the ball on a couple of "alley oop" passes.

4. Let each defender call for the type of pass he wishes to warm up on, and as many passes as he wishes.

5. Let the players perform this drill prior to returning to the locker room, before the game commences, when the players are completely warm.

6. See Illustration 142.

Comment: The pitch-catch drill is primarily recommended as a pregame warm-up drill, but can be used to advantage at any time. Many times it is advantageous to allow the defensive backs to conduct the drill by themselves. Too many regimented drills are not desirable.

FINDING-OPEN-MAN DRILL

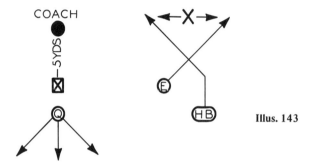

Illus. 143

The purpose of this drill is to enable defensive players to combine passing, receiving, and defense in one single drill.

INSTRUCTIONS

1. Station a center, quarterback, and two receivers on offense.

2. Position yourself downfield about 5 yards. Concentrate on the quarterback, and on the fundamentals of passing.

3. Before the quarterback throws each pass, have him first look at you, standing downfield, to simulate looking off. Next let him quickly find the open receiver and unload the football to him.

4. Tell the defensive back that he may cover either receiver. He is at a disadvantage if the passer holds the football too long. Therefore, set a time limit for the quarterback, so that he has to get the ball off fast.

5. See Illustration 143.

Comment: This is a fine reaction drill for the defenders. It enables them to practice "reading" the passer and to improve their reactions. It is, in addition, an excellent drill for the quarterback.

CROSSING-ENDS DRILL

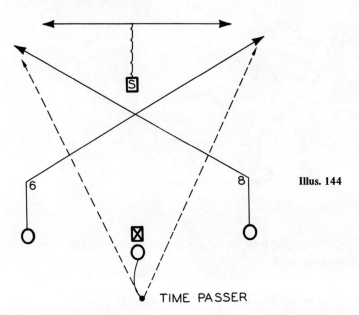

Illus. 144

TIME PASSER

The purpose of this drill is to give the safety men practice in covering crossing ends and in reading the passer.

INSTRUCTIONS

1. Station two ends, a center, and a quarterback on offense.

2. Station a safety man in his regular position on defense, 10 to 12 yards deep.

3. Have the receivers run crossing patterns, running to a point 6 to 8 yards deep before they break.

4. Set a time limit within which the passer has to get the ball off, so that the safety man has a chance to play both receivers.

5. Tell the defender that in this drill he must give ground and watch the passer.

6. See Illustration 144.

DOUBLE ONE-ON-ONE DRILL

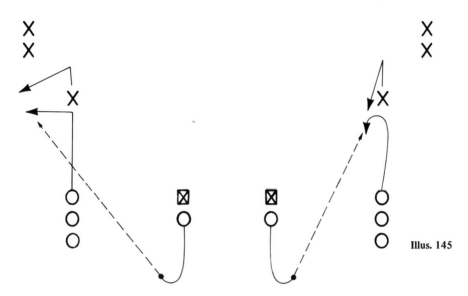

Illus. 145

The purpose of this drill is to teach defensive players all the fundamentals of coverage and pass defense.

INSTRUCTIONS

1. Station two centers, two passers, and two sets of receivers on offense.

2. Line up all the defensive deep backs in four lines, but let only two lines be active.

3. Have the receivers run any patterns they wish, but usually get them to start with the basic maneuvers.

4. Have the receivers and defensive backs switch sides.

5. Position yourself downfield to check the deep backs' stance, footwork, eyes, etc.

6. Tell the passers that they must release the football within 4 seconds from the time they get it.

7. See Illustration 145.

DOUBLE-BARREL COVERAGE DRILL

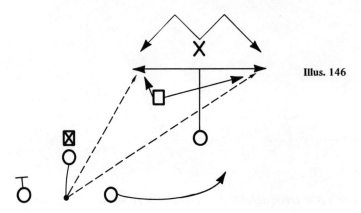

Illus. 146

The purpose of this drill is to develop teamwork between the linebackers and the deep backs.

INSTRUCTIONS

1. Station the strong-side linebacker and one deep back on defense.

2. On offense, let there be a center, a quarterback, a receiver and one or two backs. Set a time limit within which the passer must get the ball off.

3. Have the passer and receiver work on all patterns that involve the two defenders.

4. Have one of the offensive backs occasionally catch a swing pass in front of the linebacker.

5. Tell the deep back and the linebacker that communication is a must in this drill.

6. See Illustration 146.

INSIDE-OUTSIDE COVERAGE DRILL

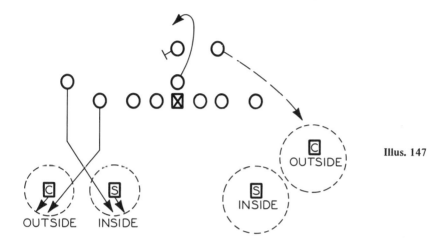

Illus. 147

The purpose of this drill is to enable defensive players to work against an offensive unit employing both a close and a wide flanker.

INSTRUCTIONS

1. Station four deep backs on defense against a complete offensive team. Use Junior Varsity personnel for the most part on offense.

2. Have the flanker on the strong side line up close to (not more than 4 yards from) the end.

3. Have the offensive receivers run crossing patterns, so that the defenders get practice in covering.

4. Next widen the flanker out to 8, then 10, then 12 yards. Have the defenders now cover the eligible receivers man-for-man.

5. On the weak side, let the corner man and halfback drill on whatever type of coverage you are teaching.

6. To provide a correct picture for the defenders, let the offensive linemen follow their usual pass-blocking assignments.

7. See Illustration 147.

WALKING DRILL

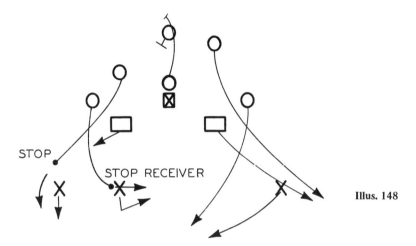

STOP

STOP RECEIVER

Illus. 148

The purpose of this drill is to eliminate, in the minds of the defenders, any doubt or confusion regarding specific pass patterns.

INSTRUCTIONS

1. Station a center, quarterback, two ends, and three backs on offense.

2. Station a complete secondary, including linebackers, on defense.

3. Have the offensive personnel walk through any pass pattern that the defense has found hard to cover.

4. After the offensive players have gotten downfield, stop the receivers and see to it that the defenders are in the correct position on each receiver.

5. Have the passer throw the football and all the defenders converge on it.

6. Next run the pattern at full speed and ask the defenders to concentrate on intercepting.

7. See Illustration 148.

Comment: This reverse teaching procedure emphasizes the importance of being in the correct position to intercept or break up a forward pass.

CHAPTER 12

TEAM DRILLS

Successful defense in football depends on the individual skills of all eleven players. *Teamwork is vital,* and good defensive play is a coordinated effort on the part of the deep backs, linebackers, and linemen.

Team drills should not be used until every defensive player has indicated that he is ready for this type of drilling. The stages of progress should include individual drills, sectional drills, and finally team drills.

This chapter includes 14 team drills. Good defensive team drills are scarce. The coach must be careful that he is using only team drills that are as valuable as the time they take up on the practice schedule.

LONG-YARDAGE-SITUATION DRILL

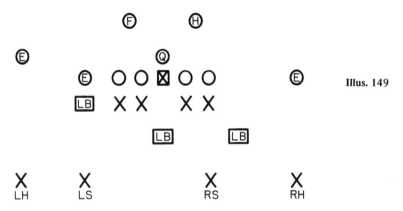

Illus. 149

The purpose of this drill is to rehearse the responsibility of each man and check the long-yardage defense on third down.

INSTRUCTIONS

1. Station a full team on defense, consisting of linemen, linebackers, and deep backs.

2. Station a complete group on offense, and have them run through your opponents' third-down plays.

3. Start out with this drill at half speed. When all players have learned their responsibilities, step it up to full speed.

4. See Illustration 149.

Comment: This drill is primarily intended to simulate a third-down, long-yardage situation. It is an especially fine drill for the defensive quarterback.

PASS-OFFENSE-PASS-DEFENSE DRILL

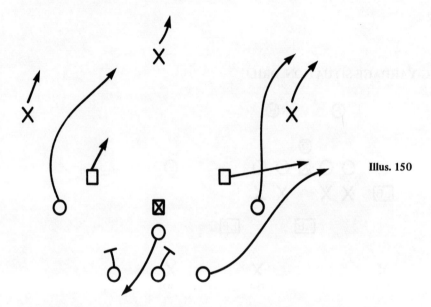

Illus. 150

The purpose of this drill is to enable both defense and offense to practice their own skills.

INSTRUCTIONS

1. Line up a complete offensive team, minus guards and tackles.

2. Station a complete team, again minus guards and tackles, on defense. Let the defense have only deep backs; or use deep backs plus one, two, or three linebackers if you wish.

3. Use the entire football field, and have both the quarterback and defensive general call signals, taking into account downs and yardage to be covered.

4. Assign one or two assistant coaches to officiate, and a manager to keep score.

5. Allow the offense to use its own passes and runs, with emphasis on the passing game.

6. Allow the defense to use its own defenses.

7. Use a scoring system that is fair to both sides. Since the offense has the advantage, the scoring must favor the defense. Here is a suggestion for scoring:

	a)	1 point for every first down
Offense	b)	1 point for every pass completed
	c)	10 points for each touchdown pass

	a)	2 points for every incomplete pass
	b)	2 points for every pass the offense fails to throw in less than 4 seconds
Defense	c)	4 points for every pass batted down
	d)	10 points for every interception
	e)	15 points for every interception returned for a touchdown

8. See Illustration 150.

LOCATING-OPEN-AREA DRILL

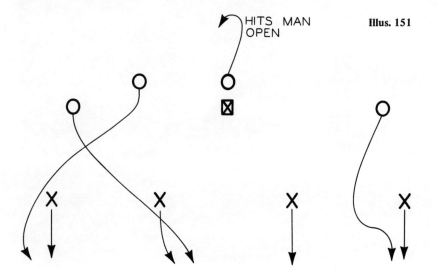

The purpose of this drill is to give all the secondary men practice in covering the entire field and in not allowing the ball to hit the ground.

INSTRUCTIONS

1. Station the defensive backs and linebackers on defense. If defensive ends figure in your pass coverage, use them also.

2. Use a center and reserve quarterback. Have the quarterback set up to pass and try to throw to an open area. Let the pass defenders try to keep the ball from striking the ground.

3. Have the defensive men use all their calls, and practice only their own defenses.

4. Tell the quarterback to drop straight back, roll out right, roll out left, and scramble.

5. See Illustration 151.

KEYHOLE DRILL

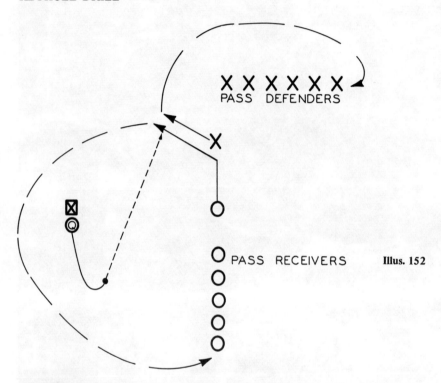

X X X X X X
PASS DEFENDERS

PASS RECEIVERS   Illus. 152

The purpose of this drill is to combine pass defense and offense and use all the backs and ends.

INSTRUCTIONS

1. Organize a pass defense team without an offensive or defensive line.

2. Use all the backs and ends as receivers. Place a center and quarterback on offense. Alternate from offense to defense: Have the offensive team work on perfecting its plays first, and the defensive team work on covering and breaking up the plays.

3. Have each offensive team huddle and call a play.

4. To keep the drill moving, see to it that the players not actually participating in the play are back behind the huddle. In this way the defender can concentrate on who is coming out.

5. Since no one is rushing the passer, set a time limit within which he must throw the ball or keep it.

6. Don't let the offense form bad habits by letting the quarterback hold the ball too long.

7. Tell each defensive player that it is to his advantage to cover as long as the quarterback has the ball. If the defenders can cover in a situation like this, they should be able to do the same under game conditions, when the opposing passer is unable to hold the ball so long.

8. See Illustration 152.

TEAM INTERCEPTION DRILL

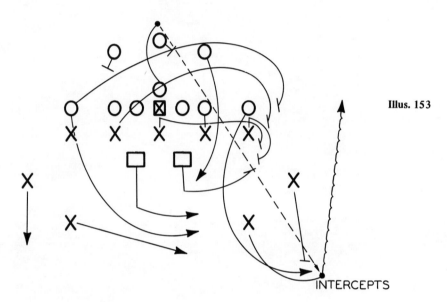

Illus. 153

The purpose of this drill is to stress defensive players intercepting the ball, and blocking by all defensive players on the return.

INSTRUCTIONS

1. Station the entire defensive team of 11 players at their regular positions on defense.

2. Use a complete offensive team of 11 players on offense. Have the offense employ all phases of the passing game.

3. When an interception occurs, let all linemen hustle back to form a picket, and let the deep backs block the nearest opposite color.

4. You can arrange to have this drill run off in three ways: (a) Full speed on the part of both offense and defense. (b) Full speed, except for the hitting of the passer. (c) Full speed, except for the hitting of the passer and the tackling of receivers.

5. See Illustration 153.

ANGLE-OF-PURSUIT DRILL

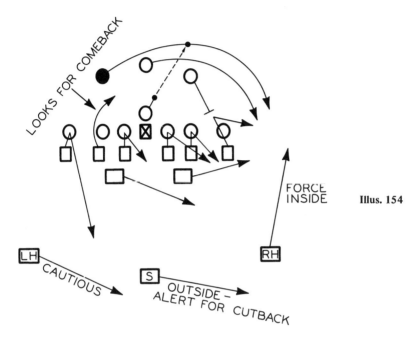

Illus. 154

The purpose of this drill is to teach defensive players the correct angle of pursuit.

INSTRUCTIONS

1. Line up a complete offensive team of eleven players, with instructions to run wide plays.

2. Station a complete team of eleven players on defense.

3. Position yourself downfield in such a spot that you can point out the correct angle of pursuit on every play.

4. See Illustration 154.

Comment: In football, players waste more energy on running the wrong angle of pursuit than on almost any other result of misjudgment. Therefore this drill is a good one for the entire defensive team because it helps players to recognize the correct path of pursuit.

TEAM REACTION DRILL

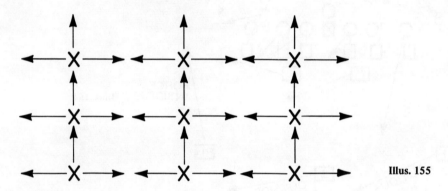

Illus. 155

● COACH

The purpose of this drill is to teach the defensive team to react quickly and accurately.

INSTRUCTIONS

1. Line up defensive players in groups of 9, with 3 rows of 3 each.

2. Position yourself 5 yards in front of the defenders.

3. When you give the commands left, right, front, back, and down, have the players react instantly.

4. Insist on precise, quick movements.

5. See Illustration 155.

Comment: This is a good drill for both the entire defensive and offensive teams.

GREEN-BAY DRILL

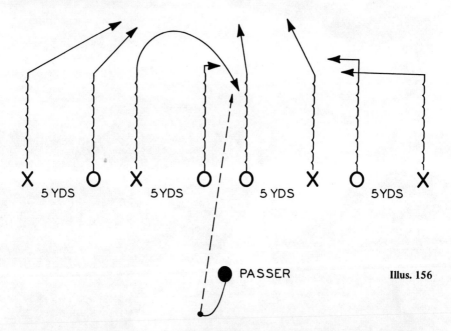

Illus. 156

The purpose of this drill is to combine all the pass defense principles previously taught and practiced.

INSTRUCTIONS

1. Have all participants in this drill put on full equipment.

2. Line up all the deep backs in their regular positions, 5 yards apart.

3. Designate one group as offense and one as defense.

4. Use an extra quarterback, and have him throw passes that are long and high, so that the defenders can get under the ball.

5. As soon as one of the defenders intercepts the ball, let his team become the offense and the other team become the defense.

6. Have the defenders now try to tackle and prevent the return, while the offense blocks.

7. You may use linebackers in this drill or not, as you wish.

8. See Illustration 156.

Comment: This drill requires at least 40 yards of the playing field. It is a good drill to use early in the season, when the squad is large and composed mostly of rookies, and it will help you to determine which of the defenders are the most aggressive.

TALKING DRILL

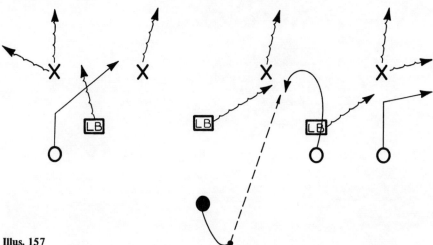

Illus. 157

The purpose of this drill is to enable the deep backs and linebackers to develop teamwork.

INSTRUCTIONS

1. Use two or three receivers on offense, with a passer.

2. Station three linebackers and three or four deep backs on defense.

3. Have the linebackers hit and charge the receivers; do not let the receivers go more than 15 yards deep.

4. Let the ends run any patterns they wish, but primarily crossing patterns.

5. Let the quarterback throw to any receiver or any spot.

6. Tell the deep backs to talk to the linebackers, because the receivers are always behind the linebackers.

7. Have everyone yell "Pass!", "Pass!"

8. See Illustration 157.

STRONG-WEAK DRILL

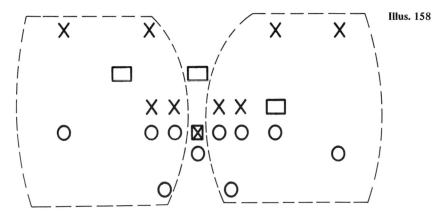

Illus. 158

The purpose of this drill is to enable defensive players to perfect techniques and specialize in specific positions on defense.

INSTRUCTIONS

1. Station eleven players on offense and eleven players on defense.

2. Designate which side of the line (both offense and defense) will be active: strong side or weak side.

3. At times emphasize plays "up the gut," i.e., attacking the middle of the defense.

4. See Illustration 158.

Comment: This drill may be live or dummy, and it enables the coach to focus attention on any area of the defense. He can watch a specific player of the defensive unit, or even watch the offensive unit. Often a coach overlooks someone because he is trying to view all 22 players at once.

LIVE-MEAT DRILL

The purpose of this drill is to enable the players to apply all the fundamentals of pass offense and pass defense.

INSTRUCTIONS

1. Station a full complement of eleven players on offense.

2. Assign a complete team of eleven players on defense.

3. Have the players run through all parts of this drill at full speed; let there be live receivers. That is, let the deep backs tackle the receivers.

4. Put emphasis on all phases of the passing game, with very little running.

FOLLOW-THE-BALL DRILL

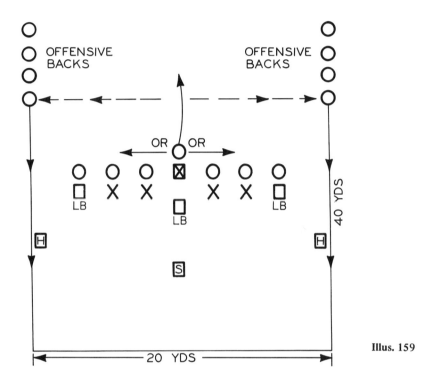

Illus. 159

The purpose of this drill is to enable the entire team to practice getting the correct angle of pursuit.

INSTRUCTIONS

1. Station seven offensive linemen and a quarterback on offense.

2. Line up eight backs on offense, four on each side, as in Illustration 159.

3. Have the quarterback, immediately after the snap, pass to one side or the other. Let him vary this by dropping straight back and having linemen rush him before he runs.

4. Correct the angle of pursuit of the defensive players after each play.

5. See Illustration 159.

Team drills   247

FUMBLE-RECOVERY DRILL

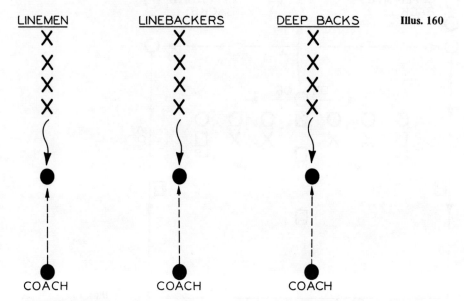

The purpose of this drill is to provide, for the deep backs and for the entire defensive team, practice in recovering fumbles.

INSTRUCTIONS

1. Divide the defensive team into three segments: (a) defensive linemen, (b) linebackers, and (c) deep backs.

2. Have one coach work with each group; if only two coaches are available, let them position themselves accordingly.

3. Have one football for each group, and let the coach throw the ball to his players, or roll it to them along the ground, simulating a fumble.

4. After the players scramble to recover the loose ball, let the coach correct any faults displayed in their technique of recovery.

5. See Illustration 160.

FINAL-FILTER DRILL

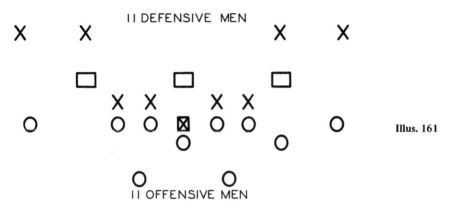

Illus. 161

The purpose of this drill is to provide a final warm-up for the offense and defense before they go to the locker room.

INSTRUCTIONS

1. Have the offense use both runs and passes that they want to practice at this time.

2. Have the defense use defensive plays that are designed to stop the plays that the opponents are expected to use in this game.

3. Let the offense run its plays at top speed and the defense line accept the blocks coming across at half speed.

4. Tell the offensive ends and backs to run at full speed and the defensive backs to cover, but to allow the receivers to catch the ball.

5. Get the players to reverse directions after a few minutes, so that the passers throw both ways.

6. See Illustration 161.

Comment: This is a good warm-up that helps timing and allows some hitting by both units before the kickoff.

CHAPTER 13

TEAM DEFENSIVE GRADING

The most difficult positions to grade, with the sole exception of the quarterback, are those in the defensive secondary, the reason being that there are so many variables as to why a pass was complete or incomplete or whether the defender had his man covered. One also needs to know whether he failed to cover his man when he was away from the point of attack. The secret of pass defense is for the defensive back to always have proper *position on the receiver.* There is an *exact* position for each defender on each type of pass thrown. The defense must be taught the correct position on the receiver for the curl, slant, out, etc.

We have used the grading chart shown in Illustration 162 to evaluate the entire team for the last six years. It is a very fair way of grading, in that the defensive men are graded only when they are at the point of attack. However, they can pick up additional grade points if they perform their responsibilities and pursue and hustle, even though they may be on the off side. Since every man cannot be graded the same, this chart is broken down into three separate areas: RUSHMEN (defensive linemen), BU's (linebackers), and DEEKS (defensive backs). (See Illustration 162.)

GRADING SYMBOLS

S	Spot (initial location)	*RUSHMEN*	
P	Point (destination of charge)	CT	Timing of charge
T	Tackles	CE	Elevation of charge
MT	Missed tackles	RA	Recovery angle
A	Assists		
SQ	Sack QB (tackle passer)	*BU's*	
HP	Hurry passer	R	Reaction (run or pass)
EE	Extra effort	PR	Position on receiver
NE	No effort	INT	Interception
OR	Obstructing the receiver		
BB	Batted balls	*DEEKS*	
AX	Axing	R	Reaction (run or pass)
BLK	Block	PR	Position on receiver
RF	Recover fumble	INT	Interception
		PP	Possible points
		PE	Points earned

This grading chart is an off-season project. It is too time-consuming to keep up during the season, unless you have enough assistant coaches to be able to assign one of them to work on it several days a week. It serves as a guide for estimating improvement as well as for grading, because you are grading strength as well as weaknesses. The best way is for one coach to grade the entire defensive team; in that way they are all being evaluated the same way. Every coach on the staff will come up with a different grade if asked to check the film. It is a big project for *one* man and at times it is advantageous to have the defensive line coach grade the rushmen and the defensive back coach the backers and secondary. Still another way is for the line coach to grade everyone with respect to runs and the secondary coach to grade all eleven men with respect to passes.

DEFENSIVE GRADING REPORT

RAMS vs. VIKINGS   Date _____   Coach George Allen

NAME	ALL PLAYERS															RUSHMEN			BACKERS			DEEKS					Final Grade
	S.	P.	T.	M.T	A	S.Q.H.P	EE	NE	OR	BB	AX	Blk	RF	CT	CE	RA	R	PR	INT.	R	PR	INT.	PP	PE	
OLSEN	-1	-2	8	1	5	2	3	1	X	X	1	X	1	1	-1	-3	-1							67	56	84%
WILLIAMS	X	X	5	1	2	X X	X	X	X	X	2	-	X							+6 / -2	+5 / -1	-	43	37	86%
BAUGHAN	-1	X	9	2	3	X -	-	X	X	-	-	-	X				+5 / -1	+3 / -1	-				62	53	85%

TEAM DEFENSIVE GRADING

Grading points: The team defensive grading form (Illustration 162) has a sample of player grading for each of the defensive areas. The manner of grading and the points awarded (or penalties given out) are as follows:

POINT STRUCTURE

S	1	*RUSHMEN*	
P	1	CT	1
T	+3	CE	1
MT	–3	RA	1
A	1		
SQ	6	*LINEBACKERS*	
HP	3	R	1
EE	+3	PR	1
NE	–3	INT	+6 (TD pass allowed –6)
OR	1		
BB	1	*DEEKS*	
AX	1	R	1
BLK	1	PR	1
RF	6	INT	+6 (TD pass allowed –6)

Awarding (or penalizing) points: To show how individual grading works out, let us take the case of Clancy Williams, a defensive back (DEEK). Note that when there is a box with an X inserted, this shows that no grade was given in that area.

ALL PLAYERS

Column		Points
T	Player made 5 tackles	+15
MT	Player missed 1 tackle	- 3
A	Player had 2 assists	+ 2
AX	Player executed 2 Axes	+ 2
BLK	Player executed 1 block	+ 1
	DEEKS	
R	Player reacted well (6 times)	+ 6
	Player reacted poorly (2 times)	- 2
PR	Player had good position on receiver (5 times)	+ 5
	Player had poor position (1 time)	- 1
INT	Player had 1 interception	+ 6

All possible points are now added up, the total here being 43, and the figure is placed in the PP column. Now all minus numbers are subtracted from the possible points and this remainder will give you the players' points earned. This figure (the total here being -6) is placed in the PE column. Now the percentage grade can be arrived at by dividing the possible points into the points earned (the percentage here being 86%).

If a deep back or linebacker allows a touchdown pass, it counts minus 6 (-6) points. If he intercepts, it counts plus 6 (+6) points. If a long pass is completed for a TD, everyone is penalized one point and the particular defensive back is penalized six points. You cannot blame just one player. If the line had rushed better, perhaps the quarterback would not have had the time to get the pass off.

SYMBOLS USED IN ILLUSTRATIONS

▢ = Blockers

◼ = Center

☐C = Corner back

△ = Defensive linemen and sometimes defensive backs

✕ = Defensive players

☐D = Dummy

☐E = End

Ⓖ = Guard (pass-blocking)

☐HB = Halfback

☐LB = Linebacker

○ = Offensive players

Ⓡ = Pass receiver

------ = Passes

Ⓠ = Quarterback

︵︵ = Running backward

——— = Running forward

☐S = Safety man

GLOSSARY

Alley oop pass: A high, looping pass thrown so that a receiver has to jump from a stopped position to get the ball.

Axing: Body-blocking a receiver as he releases from line of scrimmage.

Batted ball: A pass hit or tipped by a defensive man, usually a defensive lineman.

"Block back on": When a defensive player blocks an offensive player after an interception, he is said to "block back on" the offensive player.

Blocking cup: Protected area set up by blocking of offensive linemen (and sometimes backs) in order to give a passer time to throw.

Bootleg pass: A play-action type of pass, in which blockers move to one side of formation and passer "rolls out" to opposite side with no protection.

BU's: Linebackers (from term "backer uppers").

Cannonball pass: Pass thrown very hard with no trajectory.

"Carry" a man: When a defensive back or linebacker stays with a receiver all the way through a zone, he is said to be "carrying" him.

Centerfielder's turn: Phrase usually applied to a safety's pivot when a ball is thrown deep downfield.

Comeback dummies: Practice dummies which are anchored to the ground and which spring back after being hit.

Cover on: A defensive back's back-pedalling to cover receiver.

Cross over: To run crossing one foot over the other.

Crowbar fingers: Phrase used to describe hands of a pass receiver who has fingers "as stiff as a crowbar."

Curl (noun): A receiver's pass pattern in which he "curls back" toward passer.

Deeks: Deep defensive backs (abbreviation of "deep backs").

Deep backs: Safety men and corner men; the defensive backs.

Deep out: A receiver's pattern in which he breaks to the sideline at approximately 14 yards downfield.

"Defensing the hooks": Defensing a turn-in or turn-out pattern.

Defensive general: A defensive quarterback or play caller.

Draws: Running plays which look like pass plays to the defense, but in which the quarterback hands the ball to a waiting halfback or fullback who has faked a block.

Flag: A pass pattern in which a receiver runs toward the "flag" in the "coffin corner" on his side of the field.

Flat zones: The two lateral outside zones that are located on the line of scrimmage, three to five yards in depth.

Flow action: Action in which several offensive backs move to the same side of a formation, causing a "flow" to that side.

Forming a picket: Forming a single-file line of players across the field.

"Hang" the ball outside: Lob the ball toward the sideline for a receiver running an "out" pattern.

Hash marks: Two lines which divide the field approximately into thirds longitudinally. When a ball becomes dead at any point outside a hash mark, it is brought back and placed on that hash mark to be put into play again.

Hook: Pass pattern in which receiver "hooks" back toward passer (same as "curl").

Hook and go: Pass pattern in which receiver fakes a "hook" pattern and goes deep upfield.

In the cup: In the protected offensive area formed by blockers to protect the quarterback.

Interceptions: Passes thrown so that the defender can intercept. A *short* interception is a ball thrown so that the defender catches it while he is coming toward it. A *long* interception is a ball thrown so that the defender catches it while he is going away from it (as a receiver does).

"Key" (verb):   To look for clues or tips as to what the next play will be by watching the movements of the offensive players.

"Key" somebody: To watch him carefully, to get a tip-off as to whether a play will be a pass or a run.

Make calls: To communicate with one's teammates with words which help them to know what offensive personnel are doing.

Medium out: A receiver's pattern in which he breaks toward sideline at approximately 8 to 10 yards deep.

"Open hips":   To run with a back-pedalling type of step.

Out (noun):   A receiver's pattern in which he makes a sharp break toward the sideline after running directly upfield for a prescribed number of yards.

Out and up moves: Receiver's pattern in which he fakes an "out" move and goes deep upfield.

Outside moves: All patterns in which the receiver makes his moves toward his sideline.

Pass-block (verb):   To set up with arms bent and elbows high and stay back of the line of scrimmage.

Play-action pass: A pass that is thrown from a play which starts out as a fake running play.

Pump: Quarterback maneuver in which he makes passing motion without releasing the ball.

"Put the leather to someone":   To hit an opposing player violently.

Putting the ball away: Putting the ball into a solid holding place with the inside of the elbow against the point of the ball and the hand on the other point.

"Read" one's opponent: To study his movements, his eyes, and his facial expressions in order to get a tip-off as to the upcoming play; to "key" him.

Revolves (noun):   Plays in which defensive backs rotate either to the strong or the weak side.

Roll-out: A play in which the quarterback, after taking the ball from the center, runs to either his left or right, behind pulling linemen, in order to throw or run with the football.

Run-pass play: A type of play in which the runner has the option of either passing or running.

Running pass: A pass thrown on the run.

Ruptured duck: Ball thrown with wobbly spiral movement.

Rushmen: Defensive linemen.

Screen: Type of pass play which looks like a deep pass, in which the quarterback, after looking deep, throws pass to a halfback or fullback who has blocked and then slid out to the flat zone with the linemen.

"Set strong": A term that describes the situation in which both the tight end and the offensive backs are set on the same side.

Short out: Receiver's pattern in which he breaks toward the sideline at approximately 4 to 5 yards.

Shotgun pass: Same as a "cannonball" pass.

Side back: A cornerback.

Slant (noun): Receiver's pattern in which he slants the ball toward the middle of the field.

Statue: Statue-of-liberty play.

Stutter step: A fake step.

Swing pass: Pass to a back who has run from his position directly toward the sideline.

Throw [a pass] into the numbers: To throw a pass directly at a player's chest (i.e., the numbers on his jersey).

Tackle box: The area between the offensive tackles.

Throwback pass: A pass thrown back to the opposite side of the field.

Transcontinental pass: A pass that "travels across a lot of country"; i.e., a pass that crosses the entire field.

Umbrella defense: A specific type of defensive alignment shaped like an umbrella; an even defense, offset with two wings.

Under control: A state in which a player is in complete control of his reactions, speed, and direction, and can alter any of these instantly.

"Up the gut": A phrase used to describe a play which is designed to go through the middle of the opposing line.

"Yell one's call": Yelling "Fire!" "Tiger!" "Bingo!" or some such thing, to indicate that the ball has been intercepted and is ready for return.

Coaching staff of the Los Angeles Rams: First row, left to right, Tom Catlin, defensive backs; Ray Prochaska, offensive line; George Allen, head coach; Howard Schnellenberger, offensive ends; Marion Campbell, defensive line. Back row, left to right: Joe Sullivan, special assignments; Ted Marchibroda, offensive backs. (*Photograph by Vic Stein.*)

ABOUT THE PHOTOGRAPHS

The photographs used in this book are reproduced by courtesy of The Los Angeles Times, The Long Beach Independent Press, The Los Angeles Herald Examiner, Vic Stein, Wide World Photos, United Press International, Dave Boss, and the Los Angeles Rams.

Page xvi
Erich Barnes, of the Cleveland Browns, uses only one arm to bat down pass intended for Ben Hawkins, of the Philadelphia Eagles. Passes of this type, thrown in front of defender, often result in "pass interference" calls.

Pages 6 and 7
When a defensive player (here Jim Johnson of the San Francisco Forty-Niners) allows a receiver (Pat Studstill, then of the Detroit Lions, now of the L.A. Rams) to get more than 3 yards of vertical depth from him, the result is a completion when offensive timing is good.

Pages 12 and 13
Lamar Lundy of the Rams "tackles the ball." Dallas quarterback Don Meredith's fumble was ruled an incomplete pass.

Page 18
The Los Angeles Rams' "fearsome foursome" demonstrate "pursuit" action, which is a trademark of all great defensive teams. Left to right, Merlin Olsen, Lamar Lundy (partially hidden), David Jones, and Roger Brown.

Page 26
Many times, even though a defender is beaten, he can still reach in and get one hand on the receiver's arm before he puts the ball away. Here Pat Fischer, of the St. Louis Cardinals, wrestles the ball away from Gary Collins of the Cleveland Browns.

Page 35
Timing of the ball in flight is a skill that can be acquired only through constant practice, but it can pay off in interceptions. Here the defensive back, Jerry Stovall (St. Louis Cardinals' number 21) is on the way down as the receiver is at the apex

of his jump. Luckily for the defense, he is able to get one hand up for a deflection. Aaron Thomas (New York Giants' number 88) almost made the great catch.

Page 38
Willie Richardson of Baltimore Colts goes over for a score. Herb Adderley, Green Bay's all-pro cornerback, just missed making the stop. There is no defense against a perfectly thrown pass.

Page 45
Defensive lineman Merlin Olsen (74) of the Rams attains extra height by jumping to deflect a pass thrown by Ron Vander Kelen of the Minnesota Vikings. The quarterbacks have difficulty completing passes in situations like this.

Pages 52 and 53
Dick Bass, of the Rams, skillfully picks a hole and carries the ball for 9 yards for a first down, eluding outstretched arms of the Minnesota Vikings' Lonnie Warwick (59). Others in play are Ken Iman (50) and Carl Eller (81) of the Vikings.

Page 61
If a quarterback has time to throw, any defense is in trouble. Here Ram quarterback Roman Gabriel, protected by the Rams' offensive line, gets ready to throw. Joe Scibelli (71) moves in to take out Green Bay Packers' Willie Davis (87).

Page 69
Part of the job of a linebacker is to obstruct and hold up a fast receiver. Here Maxie Baughan of the Rams shoves Chuck Logan (number 83, of the St. Louis Cardinals) enough to cause him to lose his timing and pass route. This is perfectly legal so long as the ball is not in the air.

Pages 74 and 75
Rams' defensive back Clancy Williams drives hard and clean on Washington Redskins' John Love to break up intended pass. Williams is "playing the ball," which is what a defender must do.

Pages 82 and 83
Good secondary play entails having more than one man near the intended receiver. Here pass intended for Gale Sayers (40) of the Chicago Bears is overthrown and

Alvin Randolph (27) of the San Francisco Forty-Niners intercepts on his own 6-yard line. He then returned the ball 94 yards for a touchdown. Note that teammate Kermit Alexander (39) is right there, in a position to help.

Page 89
A linebacker's toughest job on pass coverage occurs when he is "isolated" on a fast halfback on a deep pattern. Here Les Josephson (34) of the Rams has gotten behind Doug Buffone (55) of the Chicago Bears to catch a touchdown pass thrown by Roman Gabriel of the Rams (not shown).

Page 97
An offensive coach likes to see a situation like this, but at the same time it gives the opponent's defensive coach grey hair. Here Rams' Bernie Casey gets behind Green Bay Packers' defenders for a 41-yard gain.

Page 99
Maxie Baughan (55) of the Rams is in a good position to knock the ball away as he covers halfback John David Crow (44) of the San Francisco Forty-Niners on a deep pattern. Getting a good position on pass receivers is one of the linebacker's toughest jobs.

Page 106
Big receivers like Marv Fleming (81) of the Green Bay Packers are difficult to cover; passers take advantage of the situation by throwing the ball up high. The defensive man must "go through" the receiver, shoulder high, and hit him aggressively to make him cough up the ball. Here Kansas City's Johnnie Robinson does the covering.

Pages 108 and 109
A good example of team defensive play: Rams David Jones, Roger Brown, and Merlin Olsen make Green Bay Packers' quarterback Bart Starr go into retreat by forcing him out of the "pocket."

Pages 118 and 119
Bob Boyd (40), of the Baltimore Colts, illustrates the importance of good timing. He timed this leap perfectly so that he could deflect the ball with his fingertips. The intended receiver was Gail Cogdill (89) of the Detroit Lions.

Page 127

Bulldogging pays off as Eddie Meador of the Rams continues to tackle Green Bay Packers' Marv Fleming even though ball has been fumbled. By holding Fleming away from the loose ball, Meador gives Chuck Lamson (44) of the Rams a chance to recover possession of the ball. Carroll Dale (84) of the Packers cannot react fast enough to stop Lamson.

Page 129

Teamwork is the name of the game on defense. Here, even though the Rams' Irv Cross (27) cannot intercept the pass intended for Philadelphia Eagles' Jim Kelly (84), he is able to tip the ball back to Rams' Eddie Meador (21), who then carried it 25 yards for a Ram touchdown.

Page 131

The Rams' Merlin Olsen (74) shows superb pass-rushing technique as he successfully blocks a pass being thrown by the Baltimore Colts' Johnny Unitas.

Page 138

The receiver, the Rams' Bernie Casey, protects the ball and picks up good yardage in spite of the fact that he is hit in flight by Detroit's Lem Barney. In such a situation, when the pass has been thrown perfectly, the defender can only make the tackle and stop the receiver.

Page 141

A good example of "gang tackling." Rams Merlin Olsen, David Jones, and Myron Pottios tackle Donny Anderson of the Packers, who has just made a short gain, as Jack Pardee and Chuck Lamson of the Rams close in.

Page 147

Les Josephson of Rams protects the ball properly as he is gang-tackled by Clark Miller and Matt Hazeltine, of the San Francisco Forty-Niners.

Page 154 and 155

This is the type of lateral opening a defensive team must try to avoid. Les Josephson of the Rams takes advantage of it to drive to the one-yard line of the San Francisco Forty-Niners. At right is Ram Dick Bass and Forty-Niner Stan Hindman; at left is Forty-Niner Dave Wilcox.

Page 161
Here the Green Bay Packers' pass receiver Carroll Dale (84) is covered by two Kansas City defenders, but all they can do is make the tackle.

Page 166
Once the opponent has caught a pass, the best way to make the tackle is as illustrated by Ram Chuck Lamson (44). Jam your headgear into the back of the receiver (here Gary Collins, number 86 of the Cleveland Browns) and lock your arms. Many fumbles are caused by this type of aggressiveness. Note that two other Rams are hovering in the vicinity, in position to score in case of fumble.

Page 173
A constantly alert linebacker, being in the right place by "playing the defense called," can accomplish feats such as the one shown here. Big Jack Pardee of the Rams, in a game against the S.F. Forty-Niners, has just intercepted the ball, and is now being stopped in midflight.

Page 181
The way to tackle a big receiver like Bill Truax (87) of the Rams is to get down low and lock yourself on his legs. Here Alvin Randolph (27) and Dave Wilcox of the San Francisco Forty-Niners show how it's done.

Page 183
Bart Starr, the Green Bay Packers' talented quarterback, shown in a last-ditch effort to get the ball off during a game with the Kansas City Chiefs. Buck Buchanan, in coming down on the passer, uses his great height to good advantage.

Pages 188 and 189
Constant pressure from the defensive line makes the quarterback hurry his action. Even though Bart Starr of the Packers doesn't see Rams Merlin Olsen, Roger Brown, and David Jones, he can sense their immediate presence.

Page 194
Judging the probable landing spot of a long ball while it is in flight is one of the most difficult phases of football, and requires much practice. Here Sonny Randle, of the San Francisco Forty-Niners, takes a perfect pass and makes a catch that resulted in a S.F. touchdown.

About the photographs   267

Page 198
A defensive lineman should come down on the quarterback and try to "strip him of the ball" as well as make the tackle. Buck Buchanan of the Kansas City Chiefs demonstrates good form as he starts with his arms high and comes down on Bart Starr of the Green Bay Packers.

Pages 204 and 205
A low tackle is often the most effective tackle when one is dealing with a big man. Here Ram Bill Truax goes down on a shoestring tackle made by the Forty-Niners' Kermit Alexander.

Page 213
Dallas defensive back Cornell Green rides the back of Gary Collins of the Cleveland Browns to break up a pass in the end zone. This type of aggressive work on pass defense usually results in the receiver losing the ball.

Page 221
An important part of defense is to be sure your team comes up with the loose ball. Here Rams Irv Cross and Chuck Lamson dive for ball fumbled by Cleveland's Leroy Kelly.

Page 228
A quarterback needs all the protection he can get. Here Ram Roman Gabriel has teammates Ken Iman and Les Josephson covering him from two sides; the pass was completed for a gain of 11 yards.

Page 235
An offensive back who can change direction quickly can negate the opponent's efforts even if the opponent does use good defensive pursuit angles. Here Ram Dick Bass changes his route and gets away from the approaching Lee Roy Jordan (55) of the Dallas Cowboys.

Page 241
On an end run the offensive back can often be contained by a defensive player who has the proper angle of pursuit. However, here Willie Ellison (33) of the Rams man-

ages to elude Cleveland's Bob Matheson (56), regardless of his correct angle. Ellison made a touchdown on this play, in the Play-off Bowl at Miami, where the Rams defeated Cleveland 30–6 in January 1968.

Page 246
This is an example of good teamwork making possible the "high and low" type of tackle. The offensive back Doug Cunningham of the San Francisco Forty-Niners, has no place to go but down. The Ram making the low tackle is Irv Cross (27) and the high man is Maxie Baughan (55).

Page 250
The pass receiver's dream come true: He's in the open and there's nobody on the defensive team close enough to stop him. Here Ram Jack Snow sets out for touch-down country in a game against the Baltimore Colts. Snow averaged 26.7 yards per touchdown catch in 1967.